UDANIA SMITH

My
Zeal
For Devotion

Dedication

Sweet Father: There are simply not enough words in the English dictionary to describe Your love towards me. Thank You for being immutable and patient while I took so long to complete this devotional. Thank You for choosing me.

Chris: (My love): I wrote this devotional before I met you. I had no idea that my prayer life would lead me to one of the greatest blessings in my life. You! I love you!

Momma Joann: Thank you for loving me and bringing me into this world.

Momma Gloria: Thank you for teaching me value and strength. You would always say, "Jenene, always be yourself, because the real you will come out any away." You sacrificed your life for us. I love you!

Linn: Thank you for teaching me how to pray. Your pour catapulted me to purpose. I am eternally grateful for you and your endless love.

Kisha: Thank you for always supporting me in anything that I have put my hands to. You never missed an engagement, a birthday, graduation or anything that was important to me. I love you!

Kaleb, Darion and Christian: You three are my heartbeats. Auntie will love you til the day she takes her last breath.

Kaleb: Thank you, because when I write, I can always see your face and the paper you wrote in school. I was your hero!

Missy: Thank you for being my baby. You were a huge encouragement to me, and I love you dearly.

Maggie: Thank you for pushing me in ways that caused my writing gifts to surface. Thank you for teaching me the posture of a submitted wife. I received an impartation of love from you. You are the one that I could tell all my secrets to! I love you!

WWOG (Jetuan aka Big Sugga, Felecia and Chelsea): Thank you for always praying for me and for your endless love, laughter and random acts of kindness.

Prophetess Sabrina: Thank you for taking the

journey with me. You are my voice of reason and inspiration. You are one of a kind.

Prophetess Fay: Thank you for mentoring me and carving time out of your life to teach me the ways of the Lord from a Prophet's stance.

Roslynn: Thank you for being the best Aunt on this side of Heaven.

Loleater: You are my gem, my encourager and my example of a woman who is able to accomplish the unthinkable.

Vicki and Pops: You are the spiritual parents who have become an extension of Heaven. My life has shifted because you're a part of it. I love you both dearly!

LaSheita: Thank you for coming into my life as an answered prayer. You have helped me to mature in so many ways, and you are a compilation of beauty, wealth and power. I admire you in so many ways and I love you for loving and taking care of me.

Alicia: Your love is ridiculously genuine and unconditional. There will never be another you. I love you immensely.

My Classy Godmother Von: Thank you for always being there for me and loving me the way you do.

TABLE OF CONTENTS

Prologue

Thank you for dedicating your time to journey with me as we fast, pray and delve into new dimensions in God. I would not say that fasting is easy, but I will say that it is rewarding. Fasting, as the scripture declares, is a multifaceted and multi-dimensional discipline. I wanted to give you an opportunity to join forces with some like-minded individuals who you will have the ability to touch and agree with as you uncover different facets of praying. Agreement carries weight and is extremely powerful. Listen, if God gave you instructions, be sure to find someone to agree with you and He will supernaturally cause it to come to pass. Ma'am/ Sir, I think we should grab the nearest human and obey.

There is a difference in individual and corporate fasting. This manual is written to be used for both. When I started writing this manual, my Pastor at the time (Dion Leonard) called a 40-day fast; this was as we were approaching the New Year. I was responsible for sending the congregation directives. Each day, I would sit down and pray-write. What is pray-write? I am glad you asked. It is when you transcribe and translate prayers into written words. As an intercessor and a creative, I was able to transcribe my communication to God, with God and from God on paper. Let's face it, life is so much easier when we have directions and pertinent information when we are attempting to execute an assignment, a goal or anything that requires discipline. I wrote this so you could have a written compass to assist you in prayer and fasting. See, if we're honest, we always ask so many questions when it's time to fast. Well, maybe you don't, but I do. They sound like this:

- What am I fasting for?
- Should I omit only food?
- Should I do a liquid fast?
- What scriptures can I read while fasting?
- Do I journal or take notes?
- Should I fast all day or half of the day?

Listen, I could go on and on with so many inquisitive gestures and questions. My goal is to provide you with the tools you'll need to complete a successful fast that incorporates prayer, scriptures and daily journaling. The fast can be modified. The Lord may give you instructions during the fast to omit or incorporate certain foods. This is entirely up to you or the person who has initiated the fast. Let me let you in on a little secret. Sometimes, people feel that choosing to omit foods totally makes the fast more productive. Let me give you an example of a common dialogue.

> " What kind of fast are you on?"
> "Well, I am just drinking water because fruits and veggies do not allow me to feel like my flesh is dead or that my fast is really working. I need to really feel it."

First of all, you don't measure fasting by what you feel. So, if you feel like you're dying and your blood pressure is elevated, does this please God more? Hey, I am just asking a question. Everything we do is by faith. Yes, even when we fast. Oftentimes, we hear people say, "God knows my heart." This is said to justify why some people did or did not mean what they said or did. God truly does look at the heart of individuals. This is why He is omniscient and we are not.

Renewed Mind

Week One, Day 1

No sweets
No strong drinks (sodas, coffee, etc.)

Focus Point:

- Revived/Renewed Mind (This is What We are Praying for Today)

Prayer:

Father, I renounce my will and ask that You renew my mind and create in me a clean heart. Give us the mindset of builders as You did in Nehemiah. Holy Spirit, we ask that You teach us, guide us as and help us to see through the lens of Christ. Let the Word of God permeate my mind and my thoughts. I put on the full armor of God. In Jesus name.

Meditation:

When we ask God to renew our minds, He renovates and reforms our minds. A transformation or a change must take place. This comes through the Holy Spirit and the washing of God's Word. His will must become our will. A partial surrender will not be sufficient in this season. We must become seekers. Meditate on His Word day and night. We cannot move and evolve to the future with old mindsets.

PRAYER PROMOTES THE SPIRIT OF DEVOTION.

Supporting Scriptures:

◆ **Romans 12:1-2:** I appeal to you therefore, brethren, and beg of you in view of [all] the mercies of God, to make a decisive dedication of your bodies [presenting all your members and faculties] as a living sacrifice, holy (devoted, consecrated) and well pleasing to God, which is your reasonable (rational, intelligent) service and spiritual worship. Do not be conformed to this world (this age), [fashioned after and adapted to its external, superficial

2

customs], but be transformed (changed) by the [entire] renewal of your mind [by its new ideals and its new attitude], so that you may prove [for yourselves] what is the good and acceptable and perfect will of God, even the thing which is good and acceptable and perfect [in His sight for you].

◆ **Ephesians 4:23-24:** And be constantly renewed in the spirit of your mind [having a fresh mental and spiritual attitude], And put on the new nature (the regenerate self) created in God's image, [Godlike] in true righteousness and holiness,

◆ **1 Peter 1:13:** So prepare your minds for action, be completely sober [in spirit—steadfast, self-disciplined, spiritually and morally alert], fix your hope completely on the grace [of God] that is coming to you when Jesus Christ is revealed.

Journaling:

As you go through this fast, write down what the Holy Spirit gives you each day.

Daily Reminders:

- Read the Word and ask for revelation.
- Hydrate with plenty of water/ lemons.
- Stay fixated.
- Remember your fast and its purpose.
- Protect/guard your heart.
- Guard your ear gates and eye gates.
- Rest to preserve/conserve your energy.
- Mark your prayer time on your calendar.
- Pray in tongues; this allows you to bypass your intellect.
- Always pray for your senior leaders.
- Repent daily.
- *Pray for one another*.

Humbling Ourselves

Week One, Day 2

No sweets
No strong drinks (sodas, coffee, etc.)

Focus Point:
- Humbling Ourselves/ Meekness/ Unpretentious.

Prayer:

> Abba, I renounce my will. I come boldly to the throne of grace in faith. I humble myself, and like Mary, I choose the thing that is most needful; that is to sit at Your feet. I disrobe every false way. Hide me and let my behavior be pleasing in Your sight. I am nothing without You. Teach me Your ways. I choose humility over arrogance. I submit to authority and trust the plans that You have for my life. In Jesus name. Amen. Selah.

Meditation:

> The Father exalts those who humble

themselves. When we humble ourselves, it means to be abased, bring low and to prefer others over ourselves. This is important when building God a house. Jesus is our High Priest, yet He remained humble. Humility should be worn like a garment. I love my brothers/sisters as I love myself. One of the ways to keep this stance is to walk in love at all times. What do we look like when we do not humble ourselves? We look unrefined; we begin to become complicated and sometimes rude. We should never exude behaviors that would cause others to question God's character.

HUMILITY GIVES ACCESS TO GOD WHEN OTHER QUALITIES FAIL.

Supporting Scriptures:

- **James 4:10:** Humble yourselves [feeling very insignificant] in the presence of the Lord, and He will exalt you [He will lift you up and make your lives significant].
- **Romans 12:6:** Live in harmony with one

another; do not be haughty (snobbish, high-minded, exclusive), but readily adjust yourself to [people, things] and give yourselves to humble tasks. Never overestimate yourself or be wise in your own conceits.

◆ <u>**II Chronicles 7:14-16:**</u> If My people, who are called by My name, shall humble themselves, pray, seek, crave, and require of necessity My face and turn from their wicked ways, then will I hear from heaven, forgive their sin, and heal their land. Now My eyes will be open and My ears attentive to prayer offered in this place. For I have chosen and sanctified (set apart for holy use) this house, that My Name may be here forever, and My eyes and My heart will be here perpetually.

Journaling:

Be intentional in writing. Ask the Father a question. Listen for a response. Write your prophetic word. Make a declaration.

Daily Reminders:

- Read the Word and ask for revelation.
- Hydrate with plenty of water/ lemons.
- Stay fixated.
- Remember your fast and its purpose.
- Protect/guard your heart.
- Guard your ear gates and eye gates.
- Rest to preserve/conserve your energy.
- Mark prayer times on your calendar.
- Pray in tongues, which allows you to bypass intellect.
- Always pray for your Senior leaders.
- Repent daily.
- *Pray for one another.*

Prophetic Intercession

Week One, Day 3

No sweets
No strong drinks (sodas, coffee, etc.)

Focus Point::

- Allowing the Holy Spirit to Pray Through Us (Prophetic Intercession)

Prayer:

> El Shaddai, I renounce my will. I bless Your precious name. You are good and You are worthy to be praised! You are my Rock and my Fortress, my Shield and my Buckler. Holy Spirit, speak through me so that my prayers may be acceptable as they reach the heavens. Your Word declares that You plead to God on my behalf. So, I am in full agreement with Your supplication. Teach me how to pray for the concrete structure of my church and for my leaders. Holy Spirit, reveal hidden agendas and swell up in me; take full control of my heart and my mind.

Speak through Your people! We surrender our opinions, our hearts, our minds and the fabric of our being to the Paraclete as we are fasting and praying as one body. Let there be an angelic collaboration with the angels that are assigned to each and every soul on this fast. For this is the confidence that we have in You, that You hear us when we pray! In Jesus' matchless name! AMEN! SELAH.

Meditation:

Oftentimes, we enter into prayer emotionally with nonstop requests. The power of worship eradicates those emotions and premeditated behaviors. Let us worship, enter into prayer and partner with the Holy Ghost. Utilize your Helper. Sit still and listen. Read the first line of the scriptures three times and then move to the next line and listen. Your heart posture matters.

** WHENEVER YOU RENOUNCE YOUR WILL, THE WILL OF GOD AUTOMATICALLY TAKES EFFECT.**

Supporting Scriptures:

◆ **Romans 8:26-28:** So too the [Holy] Spirit comes to our aid and bears us up in our weakness; for we do not know what prayer to offer nor how to offer it worthily as we ought, but the Spirit Himself goes to meet our supplication and pleads in our behalf with unspeakable yearnings and groanings too deep for utterance. And He Who searches the hearts of men knows what is in the mind of the [Holy] Spirit [what His intent is], because the Spirit intercedes and pleads [before God] in behalf of the saints according to and in harmony with God's will. We are assured and know that [God being a partner in their labor] all things work together and are [fitting into a plan] for good to and for those who love God and are called according to [His] design and purpose.

◆ **John 14:16 (NASB):** I will ask the Father, and He will give you another Helper, that He may be with you forever.

Journaling:

Today, write down some of the things that you would like to see in God's house.

Daily Reminders:

- ■ Read the Word and ask for revelation.
- Hydrate with plenty of water/ lemons.
- Stay fixated on Jesus.
- Remember your fast and its purpose.
- Protect/guard your heart
- Guard your ear gates and eye gates.
- Rest to preserve/conserve your energy.
- Mark prayer times on your calendar.
- Pray in tongues; this allows you to bypass intellect.
- Always pray for your senior leaders.
- Repent daily.
- *Pray for one another.*

Repentance

Week One, Day 4

No sweets
No strong drinks (sodas, coffee, etc.)

Focus Point:

- Repentance/ Yourself/ Generations

Prayer:

> Lord of mercy, who is slow to anger. We come to the throne repenting of all sins. We repent for all sins committed verbally, mentally and with our bodies. Lord, keep us during this fast and make us aware of the power of covenant. Teach us Your ways and not to adhere to our own. Cleanse us of all unrighteousness. Holy Spirit, bind my mind and actions to the cross and help me to remember Your Word. In Jesus' name.

Meditation:

> We are redeemed from the curse of the law, but grace should not be an

intentional justification to sin. Meditate on the narrative that has allowed you to agree with sin. Meditate on why you have convinced yourself that there will be no consequences for your actions. Focus on God's love and who you would rather please more than anything. Make sure you have wise counsel. Speak with your accountability partners or mentors before you decide to make the wrong decision, not after.

CRUCIFY YOUR FLESH TO LOOK LIKE HIM. YOUR FLESH HAS A VOICE, BUT THE SPIRIT IS AMENABLE.**

Supporting Scriptures:
- **Romans 5:20 (AMP):** But the Law came to increase and expand [the awareness of] the trespass [by defining and unmasking sin]. But where sin increased, [God's remarkable, gracious gift of] grace [His unmerited favor] has surpassed it and increased all the more.
- **1 John 1:9:** New International Version

(NIV): If we confess our sins, he is faithful and just and will forgive us our sins and purify us from all unrighteousness.

◆ **Colossians 3:5:** New International Version (NIV): Put to death, therefore, whatever belongs to your earthly nature: sexual immorality, impurity, lust, evil desires and greed, which is idolatry.

Journaling:

Today, write down some of the things that you would like to see in God's house.

Daily Reminders:

■ Read the Word and ask for revelation.
- Hydrate with plenty of water/ lemons.
- Stay fixated on Jesus.
- Remember your fast and its purpose.
- Protect/guard your heart.
- Guard your ear gates and eye gates.
- Rest to preserve/conserve your energy.
- Mark prayer times on your calendar.
- Pray in tongues; this allows you to bypass your intellect.

- Always pray for your senior leaders.
- Repent daily.
- *Pray for one another.*

Armor Of God

Week One, Day 5

No sweets
No strong drinks (sodas, coffee, etc.)

Focus Point::

- Put on the Whole Armor of God

Prayer:

> Lord of Hosts, I renounce my will. Your love is unfailing, perpetual, and it always gives us hope. We are a body jointly fitted together. We put on the full and complete armor of God. Let our houses be as one. Father, we beseech You to equip us with supernatural capabilities for the building of the Kingdom of God and the perfecting of the saints. In our armor, we can run through troops and leap over walls. We live in the realm of the supernatural wildfire. We declare that the love, teaching, prophetic ingenuity, deliverance and peace that we have where you have planted us will spread

continually to the souls You send to that region and beyond. In Jesus' name. Amen

Meditation::

If there is a weapon formed, there needs to be a layer of protection around the people it was formed against. The Many Breasted One has given us instructions to eradicate our adversary's plans, darts, and deceptions. He told us to suit up with His armor. He was so kind that He chose the spiritual outer apparel of the day for us.

Do you start your day without the breastplate of righteousness? Do you waiver because you have not equipped your feet with the gospel of peace? Always remember to wear your armor; this makes you impenetrable to Lucifer's devices. The weapons may form, but I declare that they will never ever prosper.

NOT ALL BODY ARMOR OFFERS THE SAME LEVELS OF PROTECTION FROM DIFFERENT DANGERS.

Supporting Scriptures:

◆ **Ephesians 6:11-17 (NASB):** Put on the full armor of God, so that you will be able to stand firm against the schemes of the devil. For our struggle is not against flesh and blood, but against the rulers, against the powers, against the world forces of this darkness, against the spiritual forces of wickedness in the heavenly places. Therefore, take up the full armor of God, so that you will be able to resist in the evil day, and having done everything, to stand firm. Stand firm therefore, HAVING GIRDED YOUR LOINS WITH TRUTH, and HAVING PUT ON THE BREASTPLATE OF RIGHTEOUSNESS, and having shod YOUR FEET WITH THE PREPARATION OF THE GOSPEL OF PEACE; [1]in addition to all, taking up the shield of faith with which you will be able to extinguish all the flaming arrows of the evil one. And take THE HELMET OF SALVATION, and the sword of the Spirit, which is the word of God.

◆ **Isaiah 54:17 (NASB):** "No weapon that is formed against you will prosper;

and every tongue that accuses you in judgment you will condemn. This is the heritage of the servants of the LORD, And their vindication is from Me," declares the LORD.

Journaling:

Write down how not wearing your armor has caused some negative reactions in your life.

Daily Reminders:

- Read the Word and ask for revelation.
- Hydrate with plenty of water/ lemons.
- Stay fixated on Jesus.
- Remember your fast and its purpose.
- Protect/guard your heart.
- Guard your ear gates and eye gates.
- Rest to preserve/conserve your energy.
- Mark prayer times on your calendar.
- Pray in tongues; this allows you to bypass intellect.
  Always pray for your senior leaders.
- Repent daily.
- *Pray for one another.*

Praying for Senior Leaders

Week One, Day 6

No sweets
No strong drinks (sodas, coffee, etc.)

Focus Point:

- Praying for Our Senior Leaders/ Shepherds

Prayer:

Adonai, how sweet You are! I renounce my will. You are the saving strength of Your anointed. Today, we intercede for our senior leaders, Pastors (enter their names). Father, grant them increased divine wisdom, revelation, the spirit of counsel and understanding. Father, give them impervious faith as You did with Abraham. Give them platforms as You did Peter; this is so that thousands may be saved and come to know You. We prophesy an unbreakable covenant between them. Let their life/marriage be a template and never a copy. We prophesy perfect health. They will never be caught off guard, because You will not have them ignorant concerning Satan's devices. Give them a divine apostolic blueprint to build with. We cover them, their vision, finances, and their families in the blood of Jesus. They are supernatural trailblazers in the natural and the spirit, and we come against and cancel all backlash, in Jesus' name. Amen.

Meditation:

Can you imagine leading people from all backgrounds who are on different levels on their spiritual journeys? Senior leaders encounter a different level of warfare. They are misunderstood sometimes, unappreciated and questioned. Nehemiah had outside opposition as he purposed in his heart to build. Come closer and look at these words. Think about our leaders who gave God a yes to the call to build. But wait, what if leaders had opposition outside and inside of the house? Can you imagine how burdensome this would be?

Put your hands on your chest and declare, "Not our house." By doing so, you have made yourself exempt from becoming a partaker of rebellion.

THE OIL FLOWS DOWN, NOT UP.

Supporting Scriptures:
- **I Timothy 2:1-4**: First of all, then, I admonish and urge that petitions, prayers, intercessions, and thanksgivings be offered on behalf of all men, For kings and all who are in positions of authority or high responsibility, that [outwardly] we may pass a quiet and undisturbed life [and inwardly] a peaceable one in all godliness and reverence and seriousness in every way. For such [praying] is good and right, and [it is] pleasing and acceptable to God our Savior, Who wishes all men to be saved and [increasingly] to perceive and recognize and discern and know precisely and correctly the [divine] Truth.
- **Ephesians 1:17-21:** [For I always pray to]

the God of our Lord Jesus Christ, the Father of glory, that He may grant you a spirit of wisdom and revelation [of insight into mysteries and secrets] in the [deep and intimate] knowledge of Him, by having the eyes of your heart flooded with light, so that you can know and understand the hope to which He has called you, and how rich is His glorious inheritance in the saints (His set-apart ones), And [so that you can know and understand] what is the immeasurable and unlimited and surpassing greatness of His power in and for us who believe, as demonstrated in the working of His mighty strength, Which He exerted in Christ when He raised Him from the dead and seated Him at His [own] right hand in the heavenly [places], Far above all rule and authority and power and dominion and every name that is named [above every title that can be conferred], not only in this age and in this world, but also in the age and the world which are to come.

Journaling:

If the Lord gives you something for your leader, write it down.

Daily Reminders:

- Read the Word and ask for revelation.
- Hydrate with plenty of water/ lemons.
- Stay fixated on Jesus.
- Remember your fast and its purpose.
- Protect/guard your heart.
- Guard your ear gates and eye gates.
- Rest to preserve/conserve your energy.
- Mark prayer times on your calendar.
- Pray in tongues; this allows you to bypass your intellect.
- Always pray for your senior leaders.
- Repent daily.
- *Pray for one another.*

Church Operations

Week One, Day 7

No sweets
No strong drinks (sodas, coffee, etc.)

Focus Point:

- Praying for Operations/ Administration/ Policies

Prayer:

Lord Jesus, we exalt Your name; we esteem You to be the head of the church. We lay down our will and declare that Your good and perfect will be done. We intercede for the operational functions/ administration of (enter the name of your church). Father, teach us to be healthy builders so that the house will be a house of order and not confusion. We declare that we have a system of divine productivity that meets the needs of God's people. We decree unhindered planning and organizing. The team will conduct, manage, achieve and execute with a high level of skill under the auspices of the Holy Ghost. In Jesus' name. Amen.

Meditation:

The health of the church is predicated on how the leaders handle different types of responsibilities. The development of a team (operations/administration) was the strategy of Jesus before He started a church. The Pastor builds the team and the team builds the Church. We are gifted people who have been stirred up to support the vision of the house. Before the leader articulates the vision, the team should share the same values. We should be sober in our expectations of the operational/administrative process. Stop moving ahead of the process of God's appointed house.

** WE DO NOT WANT AN IMPERSONAL SYSTEM AND YET PREACH A PERSONAL GOD.**

Supporting Scriptures:

◆ **1 Corinthians 12:4-7 (ESV)** :Now there are varieties of gifts, but the same Spirit; and there are varieties of service, but the same Lord; and there are varieties of activities, but it is the same God who empowers them all in everyone. To each is given the manifestation of the Spirit for the common good.

◆ **1 Corinthians 14:40 (AMP):** But all things must be done appropriately and in an orderly manner.

Journaling:

What part do you play in building? You cannot help build from a frustrated perspective. You will taint the foundation. Write about your last experiences, be they positive/negative and give them to God.

Daily Reminders:

■ Read the Word and ask for revelation.
• Hydrate with plenty of water/ lemons.
• Stay fixated on Jesus.

- Remember your fast and its purpose.
- Protect/guard your heart.
- Guard your ear gates and eye gates.
- Rest to preserve/conserve your energy.
- Mark prayer times on your calendar.
- Pray in tongues; this allows you to bypass your intellect.
- Always pray for your senior leaders.
- Repent daily.
- *Pray for one another.*

Tithing/ Financial Stewardship

Week Two, Day 8

No sweets
No strong drinks (sodas, coffee, etc.)

Focus Point:

- 100% Tithing/Financial Stewardship

Prayer:

> Jesus, we declare that You are Lord over every area of our lives. We declare that we will be a house that will consistently and cheerfully be one hundred percent tithers. We will sow seeds, give first fruits and alms. Help us to become extremely good stewards over our finances. You are the God who causes us to get wealth. Eagle's House store house will always be full. We are lenders, and we cancel the spirit of the borrower. We sow and reap. The Earth shall yield its increase. We prophesy eternal dividends. We have eternally safe investments. We are

sacrificial givers. We will never rob God. There is no lack; abundance and favor follow us. In Jesus' name. Amen.

Meditation:

In the book of Acts, the congregation was of one heart and soul. They laid all they had at the Apostles' feet. This was the New Testament Church. Could the problem be that your heart/soul is divided from the vision? If we are going to continue in the Apostle's doctrine, we must not become partial. God is the Source who extends resources to assist us. Watch this—the Bible declares that we are daily loaded with **His** benefits, not ours.

** GIVING MAKES ROOM FOR MORE.**

Supporting Scriptures:

◆ <u>**Exodus 35:21:**</u> Everyone whose heart stirred him and everyone whose spirit moved him came and brought the LORD's offering to be used for the

Tent of Meeting, for all its service, and for the holy garments.

◆ **Malachi 3:7-9 (NASB):** From the days of your fathers you have turned aside from My statutes and have not kept them. Return to Me, and I will return to you," says the LORD of hosts. "But you say, 'How shall we return?' "Will a man rob God? Yet you are robbing Me! But you say, 'How have we robbed You?' In tithes and offerings. You are cursed with a curse, for you are robbing Me, the whole nation of you!

◆ **II Corinthians 9:8-11 (MSG):** God can pour on the blessings in astonishing ways so that you're ready for anything and everything, more than just ready to do what needs to be done. As one psalmist puts it, He throws caution to the winds, giving to the needy in reckless abandon. His right-living, right-giving ways never run out, never wear out. This most generous God who gives seed to the farmer that becomes bread for your meals is more than extravagant with you. He gives you something you can then give away, which grows into full-formed lives, robust in God, wealthy in every way, so that you can be generous in every way, producing with us great praise to God.

Journaling:

Are you an emotional giver, contingent giver, or a purposeful giver?

Daily Reminders:

- ■ Read the Word and ask for revelation.
- • Hydrate with plenty of water/ lemons.
- • Stay fixated on Jesus.
- • Remember your fast and its purpose.
- • Protect/guard your heart.
- • Guard your ear gates and eye gates.
- • Rest to preserve/conserve your energy.
- • Mark prayer time on your calendar.
- • Pray in tongues.; this allows you to bypass your intellect.
- • Always pray for your senior leaders.
- • Repent daily.

- *Pray for one another.*

CONNECTED MINISTRIES

Week Two, Day 9

No sweets
No strong drinks (sodas, coffee, etc.)

Focus Point:
- All Churches/ Ministries that are Connected

Prayer:

Eternal Lamb of God, we relinquish our will, ways and attitude to You. We intercede on behalf of Apostle and Pastor Patrice Meadows and the Embassy central campus, our Aurora campus and our Pastors' spiritual parents. Father, we pray that You will release increased wisdom, favor and strength upon them. We honor them in the natural and in the spirit. Make Your face shine upon them. We declare that no weapon formed against them shall prosper. We declare that they will be lenders and never borrowers. Bless them and the work of their hands. Be a Shield

and a Buckler to them, in Jesus' name.
Amen.

Meditation:

Jesus had bowels of compassion. He was
the template for intercessors. Now that
we have a template, we will use it to pray
for the body of Christ. It is an honor to
pray for leaders and churches. It pleases
the Father when intercession is made for
those who have been set by God. The
heart posture we should have is
unwavering and consumed with love.

THE SCIENCE OF HONOR IS BEFITTING.

Supporting Scriptures:

◆ **Ephesians 4:11-16:** And His gifts were
[varied; He Himself appointed and gave
men to us] some to be apostles (special
messengers), some prophets (inspired
preachers and expounders), some
evangelists (preachers of the Gospel,
traveling missionaries), some pastors

(shepherds of His flock) and teachers. His intention was the perfecting and the full equipping of the saints (His consecrated people), [that they should do] the work of ministering toward building up Christ's body (the church), [That it might develop] until we all attain oneness in the faith and in the comprehension of the [full and accurate] knowledge of the Son of God, that [we might arrive] at really mature manhood (the completeness of personality which is nothing less than the standard height of Christ's own perfection), the measure of the stature of the fullness of the Christ and the completeness found in Him. So then, we may no longer be children, tossed [like ships] to and fro between chance gusts of teaching and wavering with every changing wind of doctrine, [the prey of] the cunning and cleverness of unscrupulous men, [gamblers engaged] in every shifting form of trickery in inventing errors to mislead. Rather, let our lives lovingly express truth [in all things, speaking truly, dealing truly, living truly]. Enfolded in love, let us grow up in every way and in all things into Him Who is the Head, [even] Christ (the Messiah, the Anointed One). For because of Him the whole body (the church, in all its various parts), closely joined and firmly knit together by the joints and ligaments with which it is supplied, when each part [with power adapted to its need] is working properly [in all its functions], grows to full maturity, building itself up in love.

◆ **1 Kings 3:9 (NASB):** So give Your servant an understanding heart to judge Your people to discern between good and evil. For who is able to judge this great people of Yours?"

Journaling:

What does honor mean to you?

Daily Reminders:

- ■ Read the Word and ask for revelation.
- • Hydrate with plenty of water/ lemons.

- Stay fixated on Jesus.
- Remember your fast and its purpose.
- Protect/guard your heart.
- Guard your ear gates and eye gates.
- Rest to preserve/conserve your energy.
- Mark prayer times on your calendar.
- Pray in tongues; this allows you to bypass your intellect.
- Always pray for your senior leaders.
- Repent daily.
- *Pray for one another.*

Intercessors

Week Two, Day 10

No sweets
No strong drinks (sodas, coffee, etc.)

Focus Point:

- Intercessors/ Corporate/Watchmen (Raise Up)

Prayer:

Abba, we honor You and reverence Your name. We renounce our will. We intercede for the intercessors, the negotiators, the arbitrators and the mediators. Let the spirit of prayer collide with their souls. Raise up watchmen in our house that will never abandon their posts. Let their character be made through You. Jesus, we follow You and Your model of prayer. Let covenant fill their hearts. Let love be a motivating factor. In Jesus' name. Amen. Selah.

Meditation:

> Prayer is the culture that should be cultivated. We launch our weapons through a foundation of love and place of prayer. Intercessors are gap-fillers as was Moses when he interceded for Israel. They have the heart of God. They receive divine invitations that allow them to be recipients of Heaven's agenda.

LET PRAYER BE YOUR STANCE.

Supporting Scriptures:

- **Ezekiel 33:6-9:** But if the watchman sees war coming and doesn't blow the trumpet, warning the people, and war comes and takes anyone off, I'll hold the watchman responsible for the bloodshed of any unwarned sinner.'
  "You, son of man, are the watchman. I've made you a watchman for Israel. The minute you hear a message from me, warn them. If I say to the wicked, 'Wicked man, wicked woman, you're on the fast track to death!' and you don't

speak up and warn the wicked to change their ways, the wicked will die unwarned in their sins and I'll hold you responsible for their bloodshed. But if you warn the wicked to change their ways and they don't do it, they'll die in their sins well-warned and at least you will have saved your own life.

◆ **Isaiah 62:6-7:** I have set watchmen upon your walls, O Jerusalem, who will never hold their peace day or night; you who [are His servants and by your prayers] put the Lord in remembrance [of His promises], keep not silence, And give Him no rest until He establishes Jerusalem and makes her a praise in the earth.

◆ **Habakkuk 2:1:** [Oh, I know, I have been rash to talk out plainly this way to God!] I will [in my thinking] stand upon my post of observation and station myself on the tower or fortress and will watch to see what He will say within me and what answer I will make [as His mouthpiece] to the perplexities of my complaint against Him.

Journaling:

Write four words to describe intercessors.

Daily Reminders:

- Read the Word and ask for revelation.
- Hydrate with plenty of water/ lemons.
- Stay fixated on Jesus.
- Remember your fast and its purpose.
- Protect/guard your heart.
- Guard your ear gates and eye gates.
- Rest to preserve/conserve your energy.
- Mark prayer times on your calendar.
- Pray in tongues; this allows you to bypass your intellect.
- Always pray for your senior leaders.
- Repent daily.
- *Pray for one another.*

Body of Christ

Week Two, Day 11

No sweets
No strong drinks (sodas, coffee, etc.)

Focus Point:

- The Body of Christ

Prayer:

Lion of Judah, we magnify Your righteous name. We yield to Your command. Help us to Shamar as well as pray. Father, heal and deliver the body. Father, make a clarion call to the church. Help us not only to build a house, but also to be strength to the body of Christ. Create in us a clean heart and renew our spirits. We are living epistles written of men. We bind and eradicate the spirit of ignorance. We ask for sound doctrine to be preached and taught. Let the spirit of excellence be our portion. We declare that its future is secure. We cover the body today in the blood of Jesus. In Jesus' name. Amen.

Meditation:

It is imperative that we pray for the body of Christ. One of the most powerful assets we have is unity. How can we grow as a house divided? The second part is to pray for the entire body. We all belong to Christ. Research what is happening to the body. What spirits do you see? What has crept in unaware? Perhaps, it is you that has smuggled pride, bitterness, anger, or strife into the church. We all play a part in the body. Check your limbs to see if they are of God. Heaven is recording.

THE HEAD GOVERNS THE BODY.

Supporting Scriptures:

◆ **Hebrews 13:17:** Obey your spiritual leaders and submit to them [continually recognizing their authority over you], for they are constantly keeping watch over your souls and guarding your spiritual welfare, as men who will have to render an account [of their trust]. [Do your part to] let them do this with gladness and not with sighing and groaning, for that would not be profitable to you [either].

◆ **I Corinthians 12:24-26:** Which our more presentable parts do not require. But God has so adjusted (mingled, harmonized, and subtly proportioned the parts of) the whole body, giving the greater honor and richer endowment to the inferior parts which lack [apparent importance], So that there should be no division or discord or lack of adaptation [of the parts of the body to each other], but the members all alike should have a mutual interest in and care for one another. And If one member suffers, all the parts [share] the suffering; if one member is honored, all the members [share in] the enjoyment of it.

◆ **Jude 4 (KJV):** For there are certain men crept in unawares, who were before of old ordained to this condemnation, ungodly men, turning the grace of our God into lasciviousness, and denying the only Lord God, and our Lord Jesus Christ.

- **Habakkuk 2:1**: [Oh, I know, I have been rash to talk out plainly this way to God!] I will [in my thinking] stand upon my post of observation and station myself on the tower or fortress and will watch to see what He will say within me and what answer I will make [as His mouthpiece] to the perplexities of my complaint against Him.

Journaling:

Ask God. Is the aroma of my worship pleasing or is it repellent?

Daily Reminders:

- Read the Word and ask for revelation.
- Hydrate with plenty of water/ lemons.
- Stay fixated on Jesus.
- Remember your fast and its purpose.
- Protect/guard your heart.
- Guard your ear gates and eye gates.
- Rest to preserve/conserve your energy.
- Mark prayer times on your calendar.
- Pray in tongues; this allows you to bypass your intellect.

- Always pray for your senior leaders.
- Repent daily.
- *Pray for one another.*

DELIVERANCE

Week Two, Day 12

No sweets
No strong drinks (sodas, coffee, etc.)

Focus Point:
- Deliverance/ The Altar Workers

Prayer:

We relinquish our will and repent for our sins. We call on Jehovah Gibbor, the man of war. You are our Extreme and Supreme Ruler. Our authority has been given by Jesus Christ. May the Holy Spirit consistently aid our deliverance/ altar workers. Let the kabowd of God be ever present. Father, cleanse each vessel that will work the altar. Remove away stony hearts and give them hearts of flesh. Let holiness be their portion and faith be their measure. Father, dismantle principalities that would make war against our house as we set the captives free. Let us move in the supernatural realm. We build, move, and plant in the strength of God. No weapon formed against us shall prosper. We will be trained, skilled and always led by the Spirit of God when handling Your beloved people. In Jesus' name. Amen.

Meditation:

If you have any conflicts or struggles with loving or liking your brother or sister in Christ, I plead with you that you do not approach the altar. The altar is sacred, blessed and should be revered, and it has been this way since the beginning of time. There will be souls that you will be responsible for. We do not want blood on our hands. If you can remember in the Old Testament, God killed men for their disobedience at the altar. The more love you have, the more power you'll have! You must establish this in your hearts forever.

Supporting Scriptures:

- **Luke 10:19 (NASB):** Behold, I have given

you authority to tread on serpents and scorpions, and over all the power of the enemy, and nothing will injure you.

◆ **Mark 16:17-20 (AMP):** And these attesting signs will accompany those who believe: in My name they will drive out demons; they will speak in new languages; They will pick up serpents; and [even] if they drink anything deadly, it will not hurt them; they will lay their hands on the sick, and they will get well. So, then the Lord Jesus, after He had spoken to them, was taken up into heaven and He sat down at the right hand of God. And they went out and preached everywhere, while the Lord kept working with them and confirming the message by the attesting signs and miracles that closely accompanied [it]. Amen (so be it).

◆ **Colossians 2:15 (AMP):** When He had disarmed the rulers and authorities [those supernatural forces of evil operating against us], He made a public example of them [exhibiting them as

captives in His triumphal procession],
having triumphed over them
through the cross.

YOUR LIFE SHOULD BE UNBLEMISHED.

Journaling:

What do you think of when the word altar comes to mind?

Daily Reminders:

- Read the Word and ask for revelation.
- Hydrate with plenty of water/ lemons.
- Stay fixated on Jesus.
- Remember your fast and its purpose.
- Protect/guard your heart.
- Guard your ear gates and eye gates.
- Rest to preserve/conserve your energy.
- Mark prayer times on your calendar.
- Pray in tongues; this allows you to bypass your intellect.
- Always pray for your senior leaders.
- Repent daily.
- *Pray for one another.*

PROPHETIC GIFTS

Week Two, Day 13

No meats
No sweets
100% juice
No strong drinks (sodas, coffee, etc.)
Unleavened bread only. (Note: you can eat fish.)

Focus Point:

- Prophetic Ministry Gifts/ Prophets

Prayer:

Daddy God, we exalt You and bow in Your presence. Father, teach us as prophets and prophetic people to master the spirit world. Mature us in the prophetic. We declare that when we prophesy, like Samuel, not a word of ours will fall to the ground. Father, we posture our hearts towards You. Father, bestow upon us boldness to utter Your words. We humble ourselves in the sight of the Lord. Teach us to discern our measure of grace and operate in that realm. Father, bestow upon us divine credibility when we speak Your words. Let Harp and Bowl flow in our services. We will not quench the Spirit; instead, we will do all things decent and in order. In Jesus' name. Amen.

Meditation:

Prophetic ministry can comfort, exhort and edify. You learn by prostrating yourself before the Lord to be who God wants you to be when you are called to any God-established office. We function and execute differently when it comes to the five-fold ministry. It is the easiest job in the world. We all have one job to do; that is to tell people what God said. When you obey God, He will highlight His Word in your heart. Of course, there are limitations. If you have not believed God for anything, don't prophesy on that level. Indeed, we are a prophetic house and have the honor of having a prophet as our leader.

Believe the Prophets and you will prosper.

Supporting Scriptures:

- **Amos 3:7-8:** Surely the Lord God will do nothing without revealing His secret to His servants the prophets. The lion has roared; who will not fear? The Lord God has spoken; who can but prophesy?

- **I Corinthians 14:3:** But [on the other hand], the one who prophesies [who interprets the divine will and purpose in inspired preaching and teaching] speaks to men for their up-building and constructive spiritual progress and encouragement and consolation.

- **II Peter 1:19-21: (MSG):** We couldn't be more sure of what we saw and heard—God's glory, God's voice. The prophetic Word was confirmed to us. You'll do well to keep focusing on it. It's the one light you have in a dark time as you wait for daybreak and the rising of the Morning Star in your hearts. The main thing to keep in mind here is that no prophecy of

Scripture is a matter of private opinion. And why? Because it's not something concocted in the human heart. Prophecy resulted when the Holy Spirit prompted men and women to speak God's Word.

Journaling:

Write down a prophetic word you received last year and pray it through.

Daily Reminders:

- Read the Word and ask for revelation.
- Hydrate with plenty of water/ lemons.
- Stay fixated on Jesus.
- Remember your fast and its purpose.
- Protect/guard your heart.
- Guard your ear gates and eye gates.
- Rest to preserve/conserve your energy.
- Mark prayer times on your calendar.
- Pray in tongues; this allows you to bypass your intellect.
- Always pray for your senior leaders.
- Repent daily.
- *Pray for one another.*

Vision

No meats
No sweets
100% juice
No strong drinks (sodas, coffee, etc.)
Unleavened bread only. (Note: you can eat fish.)

Focus Point:
* The Vision of the House

Prayer:

Lord of Hosts, we renounce our will. We repent of our sins committed against You and against our brothers and sisters. We cancel any assault on the vision of the house. Give our leaders increased wisdom and fortified strength to articulate the vision; this way, we will execute the vision in obedience, maturity and prophetic navigation. As leaders, we will carry out the tasks that have been ordained by God and transferred into the hearts of our leaders. Father, we declare that the same anointing Solomon had, according to 1 Kings 6:14, to build You a house, will fall upon us as we construct a place for all souls. We are a people who embodies spirit and skill. In Jesus' name. Amen.

Meditation:

Do you know that vision is a revelation? What is revelation? It is a manifestation, a coming and something to be revealed. It takes obedience, faith, trust and patience to carry out a vision. If vision is a revelation, then oftentimes, there will be instances where we have to wait until God reveals the next phase or the next step. The more you die to the system "self", the more your life will become like Bethel, the place where God lives. The more He fills you, the more you will be able to cover, protect, see and handle the vision as a son and not bastard. The church is built on the backs of sons. We are the ecclesia.

EMANCIPATION AIDS VISION.

Supporting Scriptures:

◆ **Habakkuk 2: (AMP):** Then the Lord answered me and said, "Write the vision And engrave it plainly on [clay] tablets so that the one who reads it will run.

◆ **Daniel 8:16:** And I heard the voice of a man between the banks of the Ulai, which called out and said, "Gabriel, give this man (Daniel) an understanding of the vision."

◆ **Proverbs 29:18 (AMP):** Where there is no vision [no revelation of God and His word], the people are unrestrained.

Journaling:

Write three things that support vision.

Daily Reminders:

■ Read the Word and ask for revelation.
- Hydrate with plenty of water/ lemons.
- Stay fixated on Jesus.
- Remember your fast and its purpose.
- Protect/guard your heart.
- Guard your ear gates and eye gates.
- Rest to preserve/conserve your energy.

63

- Mark prayer times on your calendar.
- Pray in tongues; this allows you to bypass your intellect.
- Always pray for your senior leaders.
- Repent daily.
- *Pray for one another.*

Exposing Demonic Influence

Week Three, Day 15

No meats
No sweets
100% juice
No strong drinks (sodas, coffee, etc.)
Unleavened bread only. (Note: you can eat fish.)

Focus Point:
- Our Influence/ Expose Demonic Influence/ Regional Demonic Activity

Prayer:

Most High God, we lay down our will and profess in agreement that Your will be done. Father, we pray for the region that You have set us in. We take authority and dismantle the principalities of that region. We declare that You will add daily to the church those who are being saved. Father, let the residue from every service take root in that region. Cause men to see You in every area of their lives. Father, anoint us to be great soul winners and influencers to the broken and the wounded. Father, cause men to wonder no longer. Father, bless us bountifully with Holy Spirit-filled sons/Levites. We apply the blood of Jesus over the house, the region, the schools and businesses. We cancel all demonic assignments and backlash, in Jesus' name. Amen.

Meditation:

Did you know that Peter's shadow healed people? Proverbs 16:7 says, "When a man's ways please the LORD, He makes even his enemies to be at peace with him." We have that same authority over sickness, attacks and all the powers of the devil. We should endeavor to spread the gospel in that region (surrounding our church) so that it permeates the hearts of men. God will give us influence, so make sure you don't mishandle it.

WE HAVE AUTHORITY OVER DEMONIC SPIRITS.

Supporting Scriptures:

◆ **Philippians 2:1-4:** So by whatever [appeal to you there is in our mutual dwelling in Christ, by whatever] strengthening and consoling and encouraging [our relationship] in Him [affords], by whatever persuasive incentive there is in love, by whatever participation in the [Holy] Spirit [we share], and by whatever depth of affection and compassionate sympathy, Fill up and complete my joy by living in harmony and being of the same mind and one in purpose, having the same love, being in full accord and of one harmonious mind and intention. Do nothing from factional motives [through contentiousness, strife, selfishness, or for unworthy ends] or prompted by conceit and empty arrogance. Instead, in the true spirit of humility (lowliness of mind) let each regard the others as better than and superior to himself [thinking more highly of one another than you do of yourselves]. Let each of you esteem and look upon and be concerned for not [merely] his own interests, but also each for the interests of others.

◆ **II Timothy 2:15:** Study and be eager and do your utmost to present yourself to God approved (tested by trial), a workman who has no cause to be ashamed, correctly analyzing and accurately dividing [rightly handling and skillfully teaching] the Word of Truth.

Journaling:

Who were Nehemiah's enemies, and what did they try to do? What was his heart's posture?

Daily Reminders:

■ Read the Word and ask for revelation.
• Hydrate with plenty of water/ lemons.
• Stay fixated on Jesus.
• Remember your fast and its purpose.
• Protect/guard your heart.
• Guard your ear gates and eye gates.
• Rest to preserve/conserve your energy.
• Mark prayer times on your calendar.

- Pray in tongues; this allows you to bypass your intellect.
- Always pray for your senior leaders.
- Repent daily.
- *Pray for one another.*

PSALMISTS

Week Three, Day 16

No meats
No sweets
100% juice
No strong drinks (sodas, coffee, etc.)
Unleavened bread only. (Note: you can eat fish.)

Focus Point::

- Worship Team, Psalmists, Minstrels

Prayer:

Abba Father, thy Kingdom come, and thy will be done. We intercede for the worship team, every psalmist and every minstrel. Teach them how to navigate until the glory comes. Bring critical-awareness and high-ordered thinking skills upon them. May they flow in an Apostolic divine realm. Purify their hearts and remove pride. Let divine meta-cognitive skills be their portion. Father, bless them with a Levitical anointing. Give them a heart for You and Your people.

Bless them and their families, and may
they receive Your daily benefits. We cover
them in the blood of Jesus. We cancel
backlash, in Jesus' name. Amen.

Meditation:

The ark of the covenant represented
God's presence. The Levites had the
responsibility of carrying God's glory.
Wherever the glory was, they were there
also. Worshipers should be skilled in
prayer, discerning atmospheres and must
be sensitive to God's presence; this allows
them the ability to shift atmospheres.
Their worship should never cease, like the
fire on the altar should never cease to
burn. We have to understand the power
of worship. David outlined the position,
rank and scope of the ministry of music.
The people in that era were trained to
provoke glory. David played so well that
he eradicated tormenting spirits. Worship
is not just tambourines and victory laps.
Worship is a lifestyle.

WORSHIP UNLOCKS LEVELS AND REALMS.

Supporting Scriptures:

◆ **John 4:24 (NASB)**:: God is spirit, and those who worship Him must worship in spirit and truth.

◆ **Psalms 150:1-6**: Praise the Lord! Praise God in His sanctuary; praise Him in the heavens of His power! Praise Him for His mighty acts; praise Him according to the abundance of His greatness! Praise Him with trumpet sound; praise Him with lute and harp! Praise Him with *tambourine and [single or group] dance; praise Him with stringed and wind instruments or flutes! Praise Him with resounding cymbals; praise Him with loud clashing cymbals! Let everything that has breath and every breath of life praise the Lord! Praise the Lord! (Hallelujah!).

◆ **Psalms 33:1-3:** Rejoice in the Lord, O you [uncompromisingly] righteous [you upright in right standing with God]; for praise is becoming and appropriate for those who are upright [in heart]. Give thanks to the Lord with the lyre; sing praises to Him with the harp of ten strings. Sing to Him a new song; play skillfully [on the strings] with a loud and joyful sound.

Journaling:

What are some forms of worship?

Daily Reminders:

- Read the Word and ask for revelation.
- Hydrate with plenty of water/ lemons.
- Stay fixated on Jesus.
- Remember your fast and its purpose.
- Protect/guard your heart.
- Guard your ear gates and eye gates.
- Rest to preserve/conserve your energy.
- Mark prayer times on your calendar.
- Pray in tongues; this allows you to bypass your intellect.
- Always pray for your senior leaders.
- Repent daily.
- *Pray for one another.*

DIVINE PROTECTION

Week Three, Day 17

No meats
No sweets
100% juice
No strong drinks (sodas, coffee, etc.)
Unleavened bread only. (Note: you can eat fish)

Focus Point:
- Divine Protection Over the House

Prayer:
Eternal Lamb of God, we declare divine protection over (name of your church). Everyone who enters the building shall be protected by angelic hosts and the blood of Christ. We apply the blood over the walls, the windows, every aisle, the restrooms, parking lots, offices and children's church. Father, cover us with Your skirt. Let the fire of God burn up every intruder. Let the dross come up. Let His train fill our house. Before we call, God has already answered. Surely, the

Lord will be in this place. The name of the Lord is a strong tower and the righteous shall run to it and be safe, in Jesus' name. Amen.

Meditation:

God promised to be our Rearguard and our Defense. We will not fear what man can do to us. All things will work together for His people. People who are divinely protected will never be caught off guard.

THOSE WHO ARE HIDDEN WILL ALWAYS ENCOUNTER DIVINE PROTECTION.

Supporting Scriptures:

◆ **Isaiah 54:17:** But no weapon that is formed against you shall prosper, and every tongue that shall rise against you in judgment you shall show to be in the wrong. This [peace, righteousness, security, triumph over opposition] is the heritage of the servants of the Lord [those in whom the ideal Servant of the

Lord is reproduced]; this is the righteousness or the vindication which they obtain from Me [this is that which I impart to them as their justification], says the Lord.

◆ **Psalms 91:1-2**: He who dwells in the secret place of the most high shall remain stable and fixed under the shadow of the Almighty [Whose power no foe can withstand]. I will say of the Lord, He is my Refuge and my Fortress, my God; on Him I lean and rely, and in Him I [confidently] trust!

◆ **II Thessalonians 3:3:** Yet the Lord is faithful, and He will strengthen [you] and set you on a firm foundation and guard you from the evil [one].

◆ **Psalms 34:7**: The Angel of the Lord encamps around those who fear Him [who revere and worship Him with awe] and each of them He delivers.

Journaling:

Write a protection affirmation.

Daily Reminders:

- Read the Word and ask for revelation.
- Hydrate with plenty of water/ lemons.
- Stay fixated on Jesus.
- Remember your fast and its purpose.
- Protect/guard your heart.
- Guard your ear gates and eye gates.
- Rest to preserve/conserve your energy.
- Mark prayer times on your calendar.
- Pray in tongues; this allows you to bypass your intellect.
- Always pray for your senior leaders.
- Repent daily.
- *Pray for one another.*

Solidarity

Week Three, Day 18

No meats
No sweets
100% juice
No strong drinks (sodas, coffee, etc.)
Unleavened bread only. (Note: you can eat fish.)

Focus Point:

- Solidarity—Bind the Spirit of Chaos and Confusion on All Levels

Prayer:

Jesus, the Eternal One. We renounce our will. We esteem You as the Majestic One. Father God, we pray for the spirit of peace and unity to extend inside and outside of the house. We cancel every spirit of confusion, chaos and discord. Let our words be seasoned with grace. Father, help us to be peace makers, yet be able to war in the spirit legally. Let the Spirit of the Lord break out and burn up everything that does not bring You glory.

We prophesy divine unity to be our portion. May the peace of God fill our hearts. Let the banner of God go before us. Father, send judgment upon our enemies. In Jesus' name. Amen.

Meditation:

The more unity, the more power we are fortified with. Nothing shall be impossible with God. He is our defense. The enemy loves and feeds off confusion and chaos. God would sometimes do and say things in the Bible that are contrary to what we think we know. Do you remember when God sent a lying spirit to go and deceive Ahab? Yes, it was confusing during this juncture. However, Ahab brought it on himself because of his consistent sin, worship to Baal and disobedience to God. The moral of this story is our acts of sin can leave God no choice but to exercise His sovereignty by paying the wage, which can be death. He told us if it be possible that we are to live peaceably with men. No matter how others behave, we should always exemplify the character of the Creator.

THE SCIENCE OF UNITY STEMS FROM THE AGREEMENT OF HEARTS.

Supporting Scriptures:

◆ <u>**Psalms 133:1-3:**</u> Behold, how good and how pleasant it is for brethren to dwell together in unity! It is like the precious ointment poured on the head, that ran down on the beard, even the beard of Aaron [the first high priest], that came down upon the collar and skirts of his garments [consecrating the whole body]. It is like the dew of [lofty] Mount Hermon and the dew that comes on the hills of Zion; for there the Lord has commanded the blessing, even life forevermore [upon the high and the lowly].

◆ <u>**I Corinthians 1:10**</u>:: But I urge and entreat you, brethren, by the name of our Lord Jesus Christ, that all of you be in perfect harmony and full agreement in what you say, and that there be no dissensions or factions or divisions among you, but that you be perfectly united in your common understanding and in your opinions and judgments.

- **Psalms 133:1-3:** Behold, how good and how pleasant it is for brethren to dwell together in unity! It is like the precious ointment poured on the head, that ran down on the beard, even the beard of Aaron [the first high priest], that came down upon the collar and skirts of his garments [consecrating the whole body]. It is like the dew of [lofty] Mount Hermon and the dew that comes on the hills of Zion; for there the Lord has commanded the blessing, even life forevermore [upon the high and the lowly].

- **Ecclesiastes 4:9-12:** Two are better than one, because they have a good [more satisfying] reward for their labor; For if they fall, the one will lift up his fellow. But woe to him who is alone when he falls and has not another to lift him up!

Again, if two lie down together, then they have warmth; but how can one be warm alone? And though a man might prevail against him who is alone, two will withstand him. A threefold cord is not quickly broken.

◆ **I Corinthians 12:12-13 (MSG)**: You can easily enough see how this kind of thing works by looking no further than your own body. Your body has many parts— limbs, organs, cells—but no matter how many parts you can name, you're still one body. It's exactly the same with Christ. By means of his one Spirit, we all said good-bye to our partial and piecemeal lives. We each used to independently call our own shots, but then we entered into a large and integrated life in which he has the final say in everything. (This is what we proclaimed in word and action when we were baptized.) Each of us is now a part of his resurrection body, refreshed and sustained at one fountain—his Spirit— where we all come to drink. The old labels we once used to identify ourselves —labels like Jew or Greek, slave or free —are no longer useful. We need something larger, more comprehensive.

Journaling:

Speak a word to someone today that may bring peace.

Daily Reminders:

- Read the Word and ask for revelation.
- Hydrate with plenty of water/ lemons.
- Stay fixated on Jesus.
- Remember your fast and its purpose.
- Protect/guard your heart.
- Guard your ear gates and eye gates.
- Rest to preserve/conserve your energy.
- Mark prayer times on your calendar.
- Pray in tongues; this allows you to bypass your intellect.
- Always pray for your senior leaders.
- Repent daily.
- *Pray for one another*.

Sexual Purity

Week Three, Day 19

No meats
No sweets
100% juice
No strong drinks (sodas, coffee, etc.)
Unleavened bread only. (Note: you can eat fish.)

Focus Point:
- Sexual Purity—Bind Perversion of All Kinds

Prayer:

Jesus Christ, the man God. Today, I pray for sexual purity and bind all perversion of any kind. We offer our bodies to You as a living sacrifice. Father, help us to flee temptation and to live a life that is pleasing to You. Father, we ask for strength and wisdom to be bestowed upon us. Help us to be ready as vessels that You desire to use. We pray for new members that they will come to the knowledge of truth and reverence You in holiness with their minds and bodies. We cancel generational cycles of perversion and lust in our lives and the members to come. Father, smoke out hidden agendas and predators that try and make illegal entries into our lives and congregations. We submit to Your will and Your way. In Jesus' name. Amen.

Meditation:

The enemy is cunning when it comes to this department. He will try and come in wherever there is an open door. The flesh is weak, but the spirit is willing. Many people have never witnessed men or women who have lived holy and sanctified lifestyles. Nevertheless, God will always have a remnant. The closer we are to Him, the safer we will be. If you try and do life on your own and you take your eyes off of Heaven, you will open yourself up to the devil's plots. Be accountable and stay at the feet of the Savior.

COMPROMISING SHOULD NOT BE AN OPTION.

Supporting Scriptures:

◆ **I Thessalonians 4:1-6:** Furthermore, brethren, we beg and admonish you in [virtue of our union with] the Lord Jesus, that [you follow the instructions which] you learned from us about how you ought to walk so as to please and gratify God, as indeed you are doing, [and] that you do so even more and more abundantly [attaining yet greater perfection in living this life]. For you know what charges and precepts we gave you [on the authority and by the inspiration of] the Lord Jesus. For this is the will of God, that you should be consecrated (separated and set apart for pure and holy living): that you should abstain and shrink from all sexual vice, That each one of you should know how to possess (control, manage) his own body in consecration (purity, separated from things profane) and honor, Not [to be used] in the passion of lust like the heathen, who are ignorant of the true God and have no knowledge of His will, That no man transgress and overreach his brother and defraud him in this matter or defraud his brother in business. For the Lord is an avenger in all these things, as we have already warned you solemnly and told you plainly.

◆ I Corinthians 6:18-20 (MSG): There's more to sex than mere skin on skin. Sex is as much spiritual mystery as physical fact. As written in Scripture, "The two become one." Since we want to become spiritually one with the Master, we must not pursue the kind of sex that avoids commitment and intimacy, leaving us more lonely than ever—the kind of sex that can never "become one." There is a sense in which sexual sins are different from all others. In sexual sin, we violate the sacredness of our own bodies, these bodies that were made for God-given and God-modeled love, for "becoming

one" with another. Or didn't you realize
that your body is a sacred place, the
place of the Holy Spirit? Don't you see
that you can't live however you please,
squandering what God paid such a high
price for? The physical part of you is not
some piece of property belonging to the
spiritual part of you. God owns the
whole works. So, let people see God in
and through your body

◆ **1 Corinthians 6:13-20 (NASB):** Food is for
the stomach and the stomach is for
food, but God will do away with both of
them. Yet the body is not for immorality,
but for the Lord, and the Lord is for the
body. Now God has not only raised the
Lord, but will also raise us up through
His power. Do you not know that your
bodies are members of Christ? Shall I
then take away the members of Christ
and make them members of a
prostitute? May it never be! Or do you
not know that the one who joins himself
to a prostitute is one body with her? For
He says, "THE TWO SHALL BECOME ONE

FLESH." But the one who joins himself to the Lord is one spirit with Him. Flee immorality. Every other sin that a man commits is outside the body, but the immoral man sins against his own body. Or do you not know that your body is a temple of the Holy Spirit who is in you, whom you have from God, and that you are not your own? For you have been bought with a price: therefore, glorify God in your body.

Journaling:

What is it that may make you compromise? What is your weakness?

Daily Reminders:

- Read the Word and ask for revelation.
- Hydrate with plenty of water/ lemons.
- Stay fixated on Jesus.
- Remember your fast and its purpose.
- Protect/guard your heart.
- Guard your ear gates and eye gates.
- Rest to preserve/conserve your energy.
- Mark prayer times on your calendar.

- Pray in tongues; this allows you to bypass your intellect.
- Always pray for your senior leaders.
- Repent daily.
- *Pray for one another.*

WITCHCRAFT

Week Three, Day 20

No meats
No sweets
100% juice
No strong drinks (sodas, coffee, etc.)
Unleavened bread only. (Note: you can eat fish.)

Focus Point:

- Witchcraft (the Root is Rebellion)

Prayer:

Lord God, we magnify You and praise
Your name. Father, we are prisoners of
hope. Father, we cancel witchcraft, which
is rooted in rebellion. We will not be a
stubborn people, an unloving people, a
people who sow discord; instead, we will
be sons and daughters who obey you. We
cancel sorcery, divination, poverty, lack,
confusion, black magic, white magic and
all demonic principalities from the
invisible world. We apply the blood of
Jesus. Close all open doors and protect

our houses and all who enter from familiar spirits. Let the Breaker always make His habitation in our homes. In Jesus' name. Amen.

Meditation:

Did you know that manipulation, bullying spirits and yoga are a part of the occult? Oftentimes, we hear the word witch and we think about potions and broomsticks. Nevertheless, this is not the case. The occult is real indeed. We, as believers, have to be extremely cautious of the invisible world. It truly does exist. There is an opposing force that is on an assignment to bring about our untimely demise. God is yet and still our Buckler.

JUST OBEY HIM; IT ACCELERATES BLESSINGS.

Supporting Scriptures:

♦ <u>1 Chronicles 10:13:</u> So Saul died for his trespass which he committed against the LORD, for his failure to keep the word of the Lord; and also because he consulted a medium [regarding a spirit of the dead], to inquire of her.

◆ **1 Samuel 15:23:** For rebellion is as [serious as] the sin of divination (fortune-telling),
And disobedience is as [serious as] false religion and idolatry. because you have rejected the word of the Lord, He also has rejected you as king.

◆ **Galatians 5:19-20:** Now the works of the flesh are manifest, which are these; Adultery, fornication, uncleanness, lasciviousness, idolatry, witchcraft, hatred, variance, emulations, wrath, strife, seditions, heresies.

Journaling:

Write down one thing you need to work on. Find you an accountability person.

Daily Reminders:

■ Read the Word and ask for revelation.
• Hydrate with plenty of water/ lemons.
• Stay fixated on Jesus.

- Remember your fast and its purpose.
- Protect/guard your heart.
- Guard your ear gates and eye gates.
- Rest to preserve/conserve your energy.
- Mark prayer times on your calendar.
- Pray in tongues; this allows you to bypass your intellect.
- Always pray for your senior leaders.
- Repent daily.
- *Pray for one another.*

Python

Week Three, Day 21

No meats
No sweets
100% juice
No strong drinks (sodas, coffee, etc.)
Unleavened bread only. (Note: you can eat fish.)

Focus Point:
* Spirit of Python

Education:

When we come against these spirits, we must be educated about them. Our lives must be clean. These will be driven out by repentance, fasting, praying, binding, loosing and operating in authority. Although, there is a strongman, there are also surrounding spirits. Unforgiveness can block deliverance.

Definition (Python):

This is the spirit that works against churches, families and individuals. It constricts and squeezes its prey to death. Python squeezes the life out of churches, families and people. His manifestations are weariness, fatigue, confusion, and frustration. As he squeezes tighter, financial problems begin to manifest. People leave and separate from their churches, their loved ones and this Earth because of heaviness, sorrow, grief, depression, oppression and pressure.

Prayer:

Father, we offer You a praise that is befitting for a King. We bow to the Lord, our Creator and Maker. Father, we pray that You lay the ax to the root. We ask You to sever the head of python who comes to squeeze out our potential, finances, purpose, and unity. Father, loose Your warring angels to wage war against our enemy. Father, release arrows of deliverance, in Jesus' name. Amen

Meditation:

Remember that spirits have to have an

entry point. Spirits are legalistic. If you are in agreement with them, they have the right to stay. In our prayer time, we should repent and renounce our sins.

ACCOUNTABILITY ASSESSMENTS ARE NEEDED FOR GROWTH.

Supporting Scriptures:
- **Acts 16:16:** It happened that as we were on our way to the place of prayer, we were met by a slave-girl who had a spirit of divination [that is, a demonic spirit claiming to foretell the future and discover hidden knowledge], and she brought her owners a good profit by fortune-telling.
- **2 Corinthians 2:11:** Lest Satan should get an advantage of us: for we are not ignorant of his devices.
- **Psalm 129:4:** The Lord is righteous: he hath cut asunder the cords of the wicked.
- **Ephesians 6:12:** For we wrestle not against flesh and blood, but against

principalities, against powers, against the rulers of the darkness of this world, against spiritual wickedness in high places.

◆ **Jeremiah 1:19:** And they shall fight against thee; but they shall not prevail against thee, for I am with thee," saith the LORD, "to deliver thee.

Journaling:

Do some more research on this spirit and write down other ways that it affects us.

Daily Reminders:

- Read the Word and ask for revelation.
- Hydrate with plenty of water/ lemons.
- Stay fixated on Jesus.
- Remember your fast and its purpose.
- Protect/guard your heart.
- Guard your ear gates and eye gates.
- Rest to preserve/conserve your energy.
- Mark prayer times on your calendar.
- Pray in tongues; this allows you to bypass your intellect.
- Always pray for your senior leaders.

- Repent daily.
- *Pray for one another.*

Spirit of Religion

Week Four, Day 22

No meats
No sweets
100% juice
No strong drinks (sodas, coffee, etc.)
Unleavened bread only. (Note: you can eat fish.)

Focus Point:
- The Spirit of Religion

Reflections of the Heart:
> Legalistic thinking is one of the ways we can explain religion. It is hypocrisy as well.

Definition:
> A religious spirit is a demon power that uses religious structures to entangle people in bondage to prevent transformation and to enforce the spiritual status quo. It fights revelation, defies prophetic insight and hates Apostolic authority. It also uses tradition to build structures of limitation.

Prayer:

Father, we offer You a praise that is befitting of a King. We bow to the Lord, our Creator and Maker. Father, we pray that You lay the ax to the root. The Spirit of God shall rest in our houses, regions and on everyone who enters. Lord, please sever the head of the pharisaic spirit who comes to squeeze out our potential, finances, purpose, and unity. Father, loose Your warring angels to wage war against our enemy. We will not be stuck in an old season. The letter killeth, but the spirit maketh alive. Father, release arrows of deliverance, in Jesus' name. Amen.

Meditation:

A religious mindset is not based on what you wear. A religious mindset is what it is. We should recognize it in ourselves as well. Examine your own heart. That spirit knows how to hide. We should always be praying. Reformation brings us into new revelation. Religious spirits try to block the move of God.

WE WILL NOT BE IN BONDAGE; WE ARE REDEEMED FROM CURSES.

Supporting Scriptures:

◆ **Revelation 2:4-7:** Nevertheless I have somewhat against thee, because thou hast left thy first love. Remember therefore from whence thou art fallen, and repent, and do the first works; or else I will come unto thee quickly, and will remove thy candlestick out of his place, except thou repent. But this thou hast, that thou hatest the deeds of the Nicolaitanes, which I also hate. He that hath an ear, let him hear what the Spirit saith unto the churches; To him that overcometh will I give to eat of the tree of life, which is in the midst of the paradise of God.

◆ **Mark 7:13 (NASB):** Thus invalidating the word of God by your tradition which you have handed down; and you do many things such as that."

Journaling:

> Do some more research on this spirit and write down other ways that it affects us.

Daily Reminders:

- Read the Word and ask for revelation.
- Hydrate with plenty of water/ lemons.
- Stay fixated on Jesus.
- Remember your fast and its purpose.
- Protect/guard your heart.
- Guard your ear gates and eye gates.
- Rest to preserve/conserve your energy.
- Mark prayer times on your calendar.
- Pray in tongues; this allows you to bypass your intellect.
- Always pray for your senior leaders.
- Repent daily.
- *Pray for one another.*

PLANTED

Week Four, Day 23

No meats
No sweets
100% juice
No strong drinks (sodas, coffee, etc.)
Unleavened bread only. (Note: you can eat fish.)

Focus Point:
- Planted in the House of God

Prayer:

Lord God, we trust in You. We repent for
our sins. We admonish You, we reverence
You, and we esteem You as the self-
existing Creator. We make intercession for
Your people. Father, we pray for men and
women to be added to our church daily,
and they shall be planted in the house of
God. They shall not be moved. Father,
help us not to move from Your presence,
Your Word, nor Your statutes. Strengthen
the people who will come into our
congregation. Father, let them feel the

love of God that flows through us from You. Cause their feet not to fail or stumble, but to go higher in the things of God. We prophesy to the region surrounding our churches and our cities. Let the four winds draw them to Eagle's House. Father send sons to help build the house. In Jesus' name. Amen.

Meditation :

Jesus told us that we shall be planted like a tree that will not be moved. If He said it, we should believe it. To believe means to accept as true.

THE WORLD HAS NOTHING TO OFFER YOU.

Supporting Scriptures:

◆ **Psalm 92:12-14:** The righteous will flourish like the date palm [long-lived, upright and useful]; They will grow like a cedar in Lebanon [majestic and stable] Planted in the house of the LORD, They will flourish in the courts of our God

[Growing in grace] they will still thrive and bear fruit and prosper in old age; They will flourish and be vital and fresh [rich in trust and love and contentment.

Journaling:

What are some obstacles that would cause you to be moved?

Daily Reminders:

- Read the Word and ask for revelation.
- Hydrate with plenty of water/ lemons.
- Stay fixated on Jesus.
- Remember your fast and its purpose.
- Protect/guard your heart.
- Guard your ear gates and eye gates.
- Rest to preserve/conserve your energy.
- Mark prayer times on your calendar.
- Pray in tongues; this allows you to bypass your intellect.
- Always pray for your senior leaders.
- Repent daily.
- *Pray for one another.*

DEPRESSION

Week Four, Day 24

No meats
No sweets
100% juice
No strong drinks (sodas, coffee, etc.)
Unleavened bread only. (Note: you can eat fish.)

Focus Point:
- Depression

Prayer:

Lord over my mind, I cast my cares upon You because You care for me. Holy Spirit, overwhelm my thoughts and my mind with the Spirit of God. I come out of agreement with depression and oppression. I repent for allowing depression to overtake my mind, which is in Christ Jesus. My mind is stayed upon You. My gaze is fixed towards Heaven. Father, I ask for the assistance of angelic hosts to encamp about me, night and day. I ask for the fire that burns up

everything that does not bring You glory
and everything that is in opposition with
Your Word.

Meditation:

Oftentimes, we mediate on everything
and every word that is not from God. We
never really practice true meditation.
Meditation is a technique and a skill.

IF YOU FOCUS ON IT, IT YOU CONFORM TO IT.

Supporting Scriptures:

♦ **Psalm 30:11 (ESV):** You have turned for
me my mourning into dancing; you have
loosed my sackcloth and clothed me
with gladness.

♦ **John 10:10 (ESV):** The thief comes only to
steal and kill and destroy. I came that
they may have life and have it
abundantly.
Matthew 11:28 (ESV): Come to me, all
who labor and are heavy laden, and I will
give you rest.

- **1 Peter 5:7 (ESV):** Casting all your anxieties on him, because he cares for you.
- **Proverbs 12:25 (ESV):** Anxiety in a man's heart weighs him down, but a good word makes him glad.

Journaling:
What are your strong emotions today?

Daily Reminders:
- Read the Word and ask for revelation.
- Hydrate with plenty of water/ lemons.
- Stay fixated on Jesus.
- Remember your fast and its purpose.
- Protect/guard your heart.
- Guard your ear gates and eye gates.
- Rest to preserve/conserve your energy.
- Mark prayer times on your calendar.
- Pray in tongues; this allows you to bypass your intellect.
- Always pray for your senior leaders.
- Repent daily.
- *Pray for one another.*

Spirit of Offense

Week Four, Day 25

No meats
No sweets
100% juice
No strong drinks (sodas, coffee, etc.)
Unleavened bread only. (Note: you can eat fish.)

Focus Point:
- Spirit of Offense

Definition of Offense:

> A breach of a law or rule; legal act. A thing that constitutes a violation of what is judged to be right or natural. Annoyance or resentment brought about by a perceived insult to or disregard for oneself. Something that outrages the moral or physical senses.

Prayer:

> Father of Heaven and Earth, we renounce our will and confess that Your will be done. Father, we repent first for being

offended. We disagree with the spirit of offense. We dismantle that spirit and loose the love of God. Father, we pray for those who have been offended, especially those whose offense have kept them from the house of God. We repent on behalf of every offender. Father, teach us Your ways so that we will not become a reproach to the Kingdom of God. Holy Spirit, convict our hearts for what breaks Yours. Father, make us ready to receive the people that will come from all parts of Georgia, near and far. We bind the spirit of offense and ask that You lay the ax to the root of it. Send the fire of God to purge it out. In Jesus' name. Amen.

Meditation:

The Bible says that an offended brother is harder to be won than a strong city. If you are made in God's image, it should break your heart to stay offended. We can choose to forgive.

OFFENSE IS A CHOICE.

Supporting Scriptures:

- **Proverbs 19:11:** Good sense and discretion make a man slow to anger, and it is his honor and glory to overlook a transgression or an offense [without seeking revenge and harboring resentment].

- **Luke 17:3-4:** Pay attention and always be on guard [looking out for one another]! If your brother sins and disregards God's precepts, solemnly warn him; and if he repents and changes, forgive him. Even if he sins against you seven times a day, and returns to you seven times and says, 'I repent,' you must forgive him [that is, give up resentment and consider the offense recalled and annulled]."

- **Galatians 5:22:** But the fruit of the Spirit [the result of His presence within us] is love [unselfish concern for others], joy, [inner] peace, patience [not the ability to wait, but how we act while waiting], kindness, goodness, faithfulness.

Journaling:

What offends you? How have you offended others?

Daily Reminders:

- Read the Word and ask for revelation.
- Hydrate with plenty of water/ lemons.
- Stay fixated on Jesus.
- Remember your fast and its purpose.
- Protect/guard your heart.
- Guard your ear gates and eye gates.
- Rest to preserve/conserve your energy.
- Mark prayer times on your calendar.
- Pray in tongues; this allows you to bypass your intellect.
- Always pray for your senior leaders.
- Repent daily.
- *Pray for one another.*

Healing

Week Four, Day 26

No meats
No sweets
100% juice
No strong drinks (sodas, coffee, etc.)
Unleavened bread only. (Note: you can eat fish.)

Focus Point:
- Healing & Wholeness

Prayer:

Jehovah, You are my King and Lord. We renounce our will and confess that Your will be done. You died that we might have life and have it more abundantly. We repent and turn from our wicked ways. We set our affections upon You. Father, we pray for healing and wholeness for the people in Atlanta and surrounding regions. Father, You are not a partial God. Father, let the balm of Gilead divinely spread over our house. Jesus, the Christ, we pray for inner healing for all who

come into the fold. We pray for healing
from leadership wounds, family wounds,
self-inflicted wounds, relational wounds
and generational wounds. We lift You up,
and we know that You will draw all men
to You. Father, go into the depths and the
bowels of man to root out every spirit
that may try to hide, and eradicate it. In
Jesus' name. Amen.

Meditation:

There is a place called the soul. It is where
much activity is taking place. You can be
delivered, but yet not experience inner
healing or wholeness. This is why God
says to trust Him with all of your heart,
mind and strength. He is a safe place.

HEALING IS FROM THE INSIDE OUT.

Supporting Scriptures:

◆ **Psalm 103:2-5:** Bless and affectionately
praise the LORD, O my soul,
And do not forget any of His benefits;
Who forgives all your sins, Who heals all

your diseases; Who redeems your life from the pit, Who crowns you [lavishly] with lovingkindness and tender mercy; Who satisfies your years with good things, So that your youth is renewed like the [soaring] eagle.

◆ **Jeremiah 30:17:** 'For I will restore health to you and I will heal your wounds,' says the Lord, 'Because they have called you an outcast, saying: "This is Zion; no one seeks her, and no one cares for her."'

◆ **Psalm 34:19:** Many hardships and perplexing circumstances confront the righteous, but the LORD rescues him from them all.

◆ **Isaiah 58:8:** Then shall thy light break forth as the morning, and thine health shall spring forth speedily: and thy righteousness shall go before thee; the glory of the Lord shall be thy reward.

Journaling:

Who did Jesus heal first? What was their issue?

Daily Reminders:

- Read the Word and ask for revelation.
- Hydrate with plenty of water/ lemons.
- Stay fixated on Jesus.
- Remember your fast and its purpose.
- Protect/guard your heart.
- Guard your ear gates and eye gates.
- Rest to preserve/conserve your energy.
- Mark prayer times on your calendar.
- Pray in tongues; this allows you to bypass your intellect.
- Always pray for your senior leaders.
- Repent daily.
- *Pray for one another.*

THE WORD

Week Four, Day 27

No meats
No sweets
100% juice
No strong drinks (sodas, coffee, etc.)
Unleavened bread only. (Note: you can eat fish.)

Focus Point:
- Word Life

Prayer:

Jehovah Nissi, You are our banner. We lean not to our own understanding and we acknowledge You as the Head of our entire being. Father, teach us to live a good life. Father, we pray for our cities, environments, and our houses that we are washed with the Word. Illuminate the scriptures and highlight Your heartbeats. Take our leaders deeper in Your Word so that the oil will flow down to the people who You send. Saturate us with a Word-led life. We take the Word and write it on our hearts. Make our hearts a library to store the Word, will and ways of God. Holy Spirit, teach each and every partner who comes through the doors a more excellent way to serve You. In Jesus' name. Amen.

Meditation:

We can literally meditate on His Word day and night. It is doable. We must always partner with the Father.

THOROUGH WASHING COMES FROM THE WORD.**

Supporting Scriptures:
- ◆ <u>2 Timothy 2:15:</u> Study to shew thyself approved unto God, a workman that needeth not to be ashamed, rightly dividing the word of truth.
- ◆ <u>Psalm 119:11:</u> Thy word have I hid in mine heart, that I might not sin against thee.
- ◆ <u>John 14:26:</u> But the Helper (Comforter, Advocate, Intercessor—Counselor,

Strengthener, Standby), the Holy Spirit, whom the Father will send in My name [in My place, to represent Me and act on My behalf], He will teach you all things. And He will help you remember everything that I have told you.

Journaling:

Read two chapters in the book of Psalms.

Daily Reminders:

- Read the Word and ask for revelation.
- Hydrate with plenty of water/ lemons.
- Stay fixated on Jesus.
- Remember your fast and its purpose.
- Protect/guard your heart.
- Guard your ear gates and eye gates.
- Rest to preserve/conserve your energy.
- Mark prayer times on your calendar.
- Pray in tongues; this allows you to bypass your intellect.
- Always pray for your senior leaders.
- Repent daily.
- *Pray for one another*.

LOVE

Week Four, Day 28

No meats
No sweets
100% juice
No strong drinks (sodas, coffee, etc.)
Unleavened bread only. (Note: you can eat fish.)

Focus Point:
- Love

Prayer:

You are the one and true living God. The
God who loves us with agape. Your love is
matchless. Your love bought us with a
price. Your love for us allowed You to
endure the unfathomable. Jesus, we come
as little children asking that we truly see
the love of God in Your people and that
they can see it in us. Father, we ask that
Your love arrests those who have no
church homes, those who are abandoned
and are alone. Let our houses be the
habitats of love. Let love overshadow us

and spill over to all that we come in contact with. Help us to build a love center. Father, You are the saving strength of Your anointed. Clothe us in garments of love until our families, co-workers, friends and all who we encounter are affected and drawn. In Jesus' name. Amen.

Meditation:

Agape (Pronounced: Uh-GAH-pay) is the highest of the four types of love in the Bible. Eros (Pronounced: AIR-ohs) is the Greek word for sensual or romantic love. Storge (Pronounced: STOR-jay) is a term for love in the Bible which is affectionate family love. Philia (Pronounced: FILL-ee-uh) is the love between friends.

YOUR LOVE WALK WILL BE TRIED.

Supporting Scriptures:

◆ **1 Corinthians 13:4-5:** Love endures with patience and serenity, love is kind and thoughtful, and is not jealous or envious; love does not brag and is not proud or arrogant. It is not rude; it is not self-seeking, it is not provoked [nor overly sensitive and easily angered]; it does not take into account a wrong endured.

- ◆ **1 John 4:16:** And we have known and believed the love that God hath to us. God is love; and he that dwelleth in love dwelleth in God, and God in him.
- ◆ **1 John 4:7-8:** Beloved, let us love one another: for love is of God; and every one that loveth is born of God, and knoweth God. He that loveth not, knoweth not God; for God is love.

Journaling:

Write an example of Philia love in the Bible.

Daily Reminders:

- ■ Read the Word and ask for revelation.
- • Hydrate with plenty of water/ lemons.
- • Stay fixated on Jesus.
- • Remember your fast and its purpose.

- Protect/guard your heart.
- Guard your ear gates and eye gates.
- Rest to preserve/conserve your energy.
- Mark prayer times on your calendar.
- Pray in tongues; this allows you to bypass your intellect.
- Always pray for your senior leaders.
- Repent daily.
- *Pray for one another.*

Culture of Prayer

Week Five, Day 29

No meats
No sweets
100% juice
No strong drinks (sodas, coffee, etc.)
Unleavened bread only. (Note: you can eat fish.)

Focus Point:
- Culture of Prayer

Prayer:

Merciful Father, we come boldly to the throne of grace. We ask You to stretch us in prayer. Purify our hearts and renew our minds. Father, remove all hindrances that would put an assault on us living a life that is pleasing to You or hinder our culture of prayer. Let the spirit of prayer hit our cities, regions, churches and our homes. Baptize us over again and again. Let the spirit that overcame Anna hit the people of God as they enter into our churches. We declare prayer is the culture of our churches. Nothing will be done without prayer. Father, we ask for the mantle of prayer. A life without prayer is like a day without oxygen. The disciples asked to be taught to pray. Teach us to pray, oh God. Increase our gift of tongues. It is a privilege to pray. Incline Your ear to us. We ask for a spirit of boldness to be bestowed upon us, in Jesus' name. Amen.

Meditation:

You have to stay in prayer until you want to be there. Prayer should be habitual. A life of prayer takes time, energy and submission. A life of prayer will not come without the colliding of the Word of God with your soul. A life of prayer breeds elevation. Prayer is the vehicle for communication with God. It takes you to higher dimensions and realms in God.

PRAYER IS THE VEHICLE WE USE TO COMMUNICATE WITH GOD, SO STAY FUELED.

Supporting Scriptures:

- **Isaiah 56:7:** Even them will I bring to my holy mountain, and make them joyful in my house of prayer: their burnt offerings and their sacrifices shall be accepted upon mine altar; for mine house shall be called an house of prayer for all people.
- **Nehemiah 4:7:** They all plotted together to come and fight against Jerusalem and stir up trouble against it. But we prayed to our God and posted a guard day and night to meet this threat.

Journaling:

Write down a prayer of faith. Ask God to give you a name. Pray this prayer over them.

Daily Reminders:

- Read the Word and ask for revelation.
- Hydrate with plenty of water/ lemons.
- Stay fixated on Jesus.
- Remember your fast and its purpose.
- Protect/guard your heart.

- Guard your ear gates and eye gates.
- Rest to preserve/conserve your energy.
- Mark prayer times on your calendar.
- Pray in tongues; this allows you to bypass your intellect.
- Always pray for your senior leaders.
- Repent daily.
- *Pray for one another.*

LEVIATHAN

Week Five, Day 30

No meats
No sweets
100% juice
No strong drinks (sodas, coffee, etc.)
Unleavened bread only. (Note: you can eat fish.)

Focus Point:

- Breaking the Spirit of Leviathan

Education:

When we come against these spirits, we must be educated about them. Our lives must be clean. This spirit will be driven out by repentance, fasting, praying, binding, loosing and operating in authority. You cannot get the strongman out until you eliminate his family. God can destroy any and all spirits.

Definition:

Leviathan is a family of spirits. Described as a wreath animal or serpent, he is also called the constellation of the dragon, Alnilam, Alnitak, Pleiades and Articus. His family is depression, rejection, mental dejection, UNTEACHABLE, PRIDE, STUBBORNESS, WORLDLINESS and COLD-HEARTEDNESS, to name a few.

Problems He Causes:

Problems in spiritual goals, restrictions and bondage that hinder WORSHIP, and problems concentrating in church.

Prayer:

Jesus, we renounce our will and ask that You come into our hearts. You are our strength and peace. Father, we ask that You rip and break the scales of Leviathan. We release arrows of deliverance. We ask that You lay the ax at the root of this destructive spirit. Release Your angels on assignments to do Your will. Father, we ask that this spirit be destroyed out of our churches, regions and surrounding cities. This spirit will not move me, rule me, nor will I adhere to it. Father, You give grace

136

to the humble, in Jesus' name. Amen.

Meditation:

Leviathan can affect your prayer life. People who think they do not need to pray carry this spirit. This is a covenant-breaking spirit. Hurt, rejection and rebellion cover pride. It is a protected spirit (scales). These people are hardhearted. The Word of God should wash us and cleanse us of all unrighteousness. We never want to shipwreck our lives. Only God can break this spirit.

Humility crushes pride.

Supporting Scriptures:

- **Job 41:34 (KJV):** He beholdeth all high things: he is a king over all the children of pride.
- **Job 41:15 (KJV):** His scales are his pride, shut up together as with a close seal.
- **Psalm 74:13 (NIV):** It was you who split open the sea by your power; you broke

the heads of the monster in the
waters. It was you who crushed the
heads of Leviathan and gave it as food
to the creatures of the desert.

◆ **Isaiah 27:1 (NASB):** In that day the Lord
will punish Leviathan the fleeing serpent,
with His fierce and great and mighty
sword, Even Leviathan the twisted
serpent; and He will kill the dragon
who lives in the sea.

Journaling:

Look up the definitions of pride. Now,
look up the synonyms of pride.

Daily Reminders:

- Read the Word and ask for revelation.
- Hydrate with plenty of water/ lemons.
- Stay fixated on Jesus.
- Remember your fast and its purpose.
- Protect/guard your heart.
- Guard your ear gates and eye gates.
- Rest to preserve/conserve your energy.
- Mark prayer times on your calendar.

- Pray in tongues; this allows you to bypass your intellect.
- Always pray for your senior leaders.
- Repent daily.
- *Pray for one another.*

GIFT OF TONGUES

Week Five, Day 31

No meats
No sweets
100% juice
No strong drinks (sodas, coffee, etc.)
Unleavened bread only. (Note: you can eat fish.)

Focus Point:
- Speak in Tongues (ALL DAY)

Prayer:

Father, we ask to be led this morning. We renounce our will. We come to You today and ask that the Holy Spirit lead us and guide us. Father, we give You access into the places that are hidden. Come into our hearts, minds, souls and every place that You are requesting. Free us today of all bondage. Who the Son sets free is free indeed! Father, show us our blind spots. Father, we ask for revelation. Crucify our flesh. Remove the scales from our eyes so that we can see the many facets of You.

Transform our minds and create in us a clean heart. In Jesus' name. Amen.

Meditation:

Manifold, deep, difference, several and many. We have 27 letters that represent the entire world, country and nation. Let's say we want to pray for the government in every nation. We can go to those places in our heavenly language. Direct your prayer even before you start. When speaking in tongues, you're open and God is pouring out principles. Praying in tongues is not just to sound deep, but God expects something from us.

TONGUES ERADICATE YOUR INTELLECT.

Supporting Scriptures:

◆ <u>1 Corinthians 14:2:</u> For he that speaketh in an unknown tongue speaketh not unto men, but unto God: for no man understandeth him; howbeit in the spirit he speaketh mysteries.

- **Romans 8:26-27:** Likewise the Spirit also helpeth our infirmities: for we know not what we should pray for as we ought: but the Spirit itself maketh intercession for us with groanings which cannot be uttered And he that searcheth the hearts knoweth what is the mind of the Spirit, because he maketh intercession for the saints according to the will of God.
- **1 Corinthians 14:18:** I thank God that I speak in [unknown] tongues more than all of you.

Journaling:

What is God saying to you in this season?

Daily Reminders:

- Read the Word and ask for revelation.
- Hydrate with plenty of water/ lemons.
- Stay fixated on Jesus.
- Remember your fast and its purpose.
- Protect/guard your heart.
- Guard your ear gates and eye gates.
- Rest to preserve/conserve your energy.
- Mark prayer times on your calendar.

- Pray in tongues; this allows you to bypass your intellect.
- Always pray for your senior leaders.
- Repent daily.
- *Pray for one another.*

Individual Prayer

Week Five, Day 32

No meats
No sweets
100% juice
No strong drinks (sodas, coffee, etc.)
Unleavened bread only. (Note: you can eat fish.)

Focus Point:

- Place Names of Specific Individuals Here

Prayer:

Father, we lift up these vessels of honor unto You. Father, cause there to be a quickening in each of their lives. Father, cause their ears to be at Heaven's door. Father, You are the Creator of all things. So, as You spoke in Genesis, "Let there be," we prophesy, let there be a shift in their businesses until their income triples; let there be joy that comes from streams of living water in their lives, let there be platforms for them to stand on, and let there be a shift in their mindsets. Let the spirit of the Levite arrest the men of God. Father, give them all excellent spirits and cause them to walk in wisdom as they build You a house. Father, let the people who enter Your house see Jesus in every one of us. Let unity be their portion. You know the hairs on their heads. Let them house Your glory. Create in them clean hearts and renew their spirits. Let them walk in faithfulness to the ministry and remember Your covenant, in Jesus' name. Amen.

Meditation:

How do you know when you have forgiven? When you are able to cry out before the Master in prayer on their behalves. We were made in His image. What image do you portray? His or yours? Make sure you choose the right image consultant. We are one.

**YOU CANNOT PRAY FOR PEOPLE YOU DO NOT FORGIVE; YOU FORFEIT THE RIGHT TO DO SO THE MINUTE YOU

CHOOSE TO REMAIN IN UNFORGIVENESS.**

Supporting Scriptures:

+ **Luke 22:32:** But I have prayed [especially] for you [Peter], that your faith [and confidence in Me] may not fail; and you, once you have turned back again [to Me], strengthen and support your brothers [in the faith]."

+ **Proverbs 27:17:** As iron sharpens iron, so one man sharpens [and influences] another [through discussion].

+ **Psalm 91:1:** He who dwells in the shelter of the Most High will remain secure and rest in the shadow of the Almighty [whose power no enemy can withstand].

+ **Isaiah 54:17:** No weapon that is formed against thee shall prosper; and every tongue that shall rise against thee in judgment thou shalt condemn. This is the heritage of the servants of the LORD, and their righteousness is of me, saith the LORD.

Journaling:

> Text each one of them a decree or a word that the Lord gives you.

Daily Reminders:

- Read the Word and ask for revelation.
- Hydrate with plenty of water/ lemons.
- Stay fixated on Jesus.
- Remember your fast and its purpose.
- Protect/guard your heart.
- Guard your ear gates and eye gates.
- Rest to preserve/conserve your energy.
- Mark prayer times on your calendar.
- Pray in tongues; this allows you to bypass your intellect.
- Always pray for your senior leaders.
- Repent daily.
- *Pray for one another.*

Prayers for Various People

No meats
No sweets
100% juice
No strong drinks (sodas, coffee, etc.)
Unleavened bread only. (Note: you can eat fish.)

Focus Point:

- Place Names of Specific Individuals

Prayer:

> Abba, we renounce our will as we lift up
> these blessed women unto you. Father,
> we ask for a glory shift in their prayer
> lives. Father, we decree that they will fulfill
> their assignments as they build God a
> house. We pray that barriers are torn
> down. We pray that every restriction be
> removed. No weapon formed against
> them shall prosper. Father, let there be a
> birthing of purpose in each of their lives.
> Let the supernatural move of God be their
> portion. Let the spirit of prayer come

upon each of them. Deliver, heal, and make them whole. Father, cause them to see in the spirit. Let wisdom be bestowed upon them. Sprinkle them with clean water. Holy Spirit, arrest them. In Jesus' name. Amen.

Meditation:

We are mandated to pray for one another without ceasing. There is power in agreement. Prayer is a lifestyle. The Holy Spirit will give us direction. Let's move from low-level prayers to high-level prayers. Once you have moved from your priestly anointing, raise up and begin to decree in your Kingly anointing. We never cease to pray.

WE ARE TRI-PART BEINGS.

Supporting Scriptures:

- ◆ **1 Corinthians 13:7:** Beareth all things, believeth all things, hopeth all things, endureth all things.
- ◆ **Daniel 11:32:** And such as do wickedly

against the covenant shall he corrupt by flatteries: but the people that do know their God shall be strong and do exploits.

◆ **Daniel 5:12:** Forasmuch as an excellent spirit, and knowledge, and understanding, interpreting of dreams, and shewing of hard sentences, and dissolving of doubts, were found in the same Daniel, whom the king named Belteshazzar: now let Daniel be called, and he will shew the interpretation.

◆ **Isaiah 54:17:** No weapon that is formed against thee shall prosper; and every tongue that shall rise against thee in judgment thou shalt condemn. This is the heritage of the servants of the LORD, and their righteousness is of me, saith the LORD.

Journaling:

Text each one of them and give them a word or send them some love. Be led by God.

Daily Reminders:

- Read the Word and ask for revelation.
- Hydrate with plenty of water/ lemons.
- Stay fixated on Jesus.
- Remember your fast and its purpose.
- Protect/guard your heart.
- Guard your ear gates and eye gates.
- Rest to preserve/conserve your energy.
- Mark prayer times on your calendar.
- Pray in tongues; this allows you to bypass your intellect.
- Always pray for your senior leaders.
- Repent daily.
- *Pray for one another.*

7 Mountains

Week Five, Day 34

No meats
No sweets
100% juice
No strong drinks (sodas, coffee, etc.)
Unleavened bread only. (Note: you can eat fish.)

Focus Point:
- Seven Mountains of GOD

Prayer:

Lord Jesus, we approach the throne of grace humbly as we make intercession for the seven mountains of influence, which are:
- Government
- Media
- Entertainment
- Arts & Entertainment
- Education
- Religion
- Family

We ask that You send Your consuming fire to burn up anything that has evil influence and intent. Breathe on every mountain and dispatch Your angels to garrison each one. Raise men up and sit men down. Close doors and divinely open those that should be opened. Expose the enemy in every area. Turn the hearts of men towards You. Protect our children and govern their exposure. Raise up men and women chosen from Heaven's information bank to come forth in every mountain. Let unity move forward in righteousness, in Jesus' name .Amen.

Meditation:

Intercessory prayer is selfless. It is a position that you take irrespective of opinions. If we are crucified with Him, why are we so judgmental? Why is it that we cannot control our tongues? Do we have to be right all the time? God loves humility. Let's meditate on looking, talking and serving more like Him daily.

IF YOU DECLARE THE DECREE, YOU ARE IN ALIGNMENT WITH AUTHORITY.

Supporting Scriptures:

◆ **1 Timothy 2:1-3 (NIV):** I urge, then, first of all, that petitions, prayers, intercession and thanksgiving be made for all people — for kings and all those in authority, that we may live peaceful and quiet lives in all godliness and holiness. This is good, and pleases God our Savior.

◆ **Proverbs 21:1 (AMP):** The king's heart is like channels of water in the hand of the LORD; He turns it whichever way He wishes.

Journaling:

Choose one mountain and, either with your talent, time or finance, sow into it any way the Lord leads you. Journal it with a date.

Daily Reminders:

■ Read the Word and ask for revelation.

- Hydrate with plenty of water/ lemons.
- Stay fixated on Jesus.
- Remember your fast and its purpose.
- Protect/guard your heart.
- Guard your ear gates and eye gates.
- Rest to preserve/conserve your energy.
- Mark prayer times on your calendar.
- Pray in tongues; this allows you to bypass your intellect.
- Always pray for your senior leaders.
- Repent daily.
- *Pray for one another.*

100 Souls

Week Five, Day 35 (3 days)

Fruits and veggies only

No meats

No sweets

100% juice

No strong drinks (sodas, coffee, etc.)

Unleavened bread only. (Note: you can eat fish.)

Focus Point:
- 100 Souls

Prayer:

>Father, today we stand in agreement for one hundred souls. No man comes to the Father unless You draw them. Father, let there be a supernatural shift. Father, we welcome the broken, lost, wounded and those who will be able to add to our house. Touch the hearts of the people and call them in from the North, South, East and West. We pray for those who cry out looking for a place of refuge. We pray for the reconciliation of those souls to be

sent to Eagle House. Lord, let Your glory rest upon our house that the men and women of God will hunger and thirst after You. We come against every hindrance that would block the people of God from entering into Your house. Father, charge the angels and assign them to these souls. No weapon formed against them shall prosper. We are in full agreement. In Jesus' Name. Amen.

Meditation:

Does your life outside of church make people want to follow you and visit your church? When people see you on social media, what do you think would be the first word they'd use to describe you? Someone is always watching us. We are living epistles. The way we live shows. Let's live a life that is a magnet for souls.

YOU MUST FIRST LIFT HIM, AND HE WILL DRAW NEAR.

Supporting Scriptures:

- **Acts 2:47:** Praising God and having favour with all the people. And the Lord added to the church daily such as should be saved.
- **Proverbs 11:30:** The fruit of the righteous is a tree of life; and he that winneth souls is wise.
- **Acts 2:41:** Then they that gladly received his word were baptized: and the same day there were added unto them about three thousand souls.

Journaling:

Make a list of people that you can invite to church.

Daily Reminders:

- Read the Word and ask for revelation.
- Hydrate with plenty of water/ lemons.
- Stay fixated on Jesus.
- Remember your fast and its purpose.
- Protect/guard your heart.
- Guard your ear gates and eye gates.
- Rest to preserve/conserve your energy.

- Mark prayer times on your calendar.
- Pray in tongues; this allows you to bypass your intellect.
- Always pray for your senior leaders.
- Repent daily.
- *Pray for one another.*

Divine Perspective

Week Five, Day 36 (3 days)

Fruits and veggies only
No meats
No sweets
100% juice
No strong drinks (sodas, coffee, etc.)
Unleavened bread only. (Note: you can eat fish.)

Focus Point::

- A Divine Perspective Shift

Prayer:

Lord of Hosts, we bless Your name and magnIfy You. We enter ınto Your presence casting our crowns before You. Father, we ask for a divine shift in our perspectives and the way we see our churches, people and our current situations. We ask for wisdom and clarity. Remove the scales from our eyes. Help us to see as You see. We walk by faith and not by sight. We have the mind of Christ, so we choose to use it today. Activate us today. Help us to see our churches filled with believers and spiritual Boaz's. Help us to get prepared for every prophetic word You have spoken. Purify our outlook, our point of views and our perspectives. Holy Spirit, be a teacher today. We invoke Your assistance. In Jesus' name. Amen.

Definition:

A mental view or prospect. The interrelation in which a subject or its parts are mentally viewed. The appearance to the eye of objects in respect to their relative distance and positions.

Meditation:

When we look at situations, we have to look at them from a faith perspective. It really is not always what it seems. We already have the victory. God has already done everything He was supposed to do before the foundation of the world. We have to get to work. We have to move by faith and not by how and what we see. This is why David asked God to "renew the right spirit in him". This is why we are to be "transformed by the renewing of our minds." God would always say "let there be"! The word **be** means to have identity with; to constitute the same idea or object as.

YOUR OUTLOOK CAN CHANGE YOUR ATTITUDE.

Supporting Scriptures:
- **Colossians 3:2 (NASB):** Set your mind on the things above, not on the things that are on earth.
- **1 Peter 5:8 (NASB):** Be of sober spirit, be on the alert. Your adversary, the devil, prowls around like a roaring lion, seeking someone to devour.
- **Psalm 73:26 (NASB):** My flesh and my heart may fail, but God is the strength of my heart and my portion forever.
- **Philippians 1:23 (NASB):** But I am hard-pressed from both directions, having

the desire to depart and be with Christ, for that is very much better.

Journaling:

Find a scripture that encourages your perspective and quote/meditate on it all day.

Daily Reminders:

- ■ Read the Word and ask for revelation.
- Hydrate with plenty of water/ lemons.
- Stay fixated on Jesus.
- Remember your fast and its purpose.
- Protect/guard your heart.
- Guard your ear gates and eye gates.
- Rest to preserve/conserve your energy.
- Mark prayer times on your calendar.
- Pray in tongues; this allows you to bypass your intellect.
- Always pray for your senior leaders.
- Repent daily.
- *Pray for one another.*

Maturity

Week Five, Day 37

Fruits and veggies only
No meats
No sweets
100% juice
No strong drinks (sodas, coffee, etc.)
Unleavened bread only. (Note: you can eat fish.)

Focus Point:

- Maturity (in the Word, emotions, approach and response.)

Prayer:

Counselor, Revelation and Bread of Life, I beseech You to teach me the way of maturity in the Word, in my life, in decision-making, in my finances, in my giving, in my prayer life, in my choices, and as a husband, wife, woman, man, teen, Pastor, entrepreneur, teacher, or student. I declare that I will not be developmentally delayed, held back, tricked, blinded or be bound by anything that is in opposition to my growth in every area of my life. I ask to be led and taught by the Holy Spirit and I relinquish control unto You, in Jesus' name. Amen.

Meditation:

The word perfect means to mature. One's life is made up of many stages. These stages are filled with lessons, levels, experiences, times, seasons, growths, wins, losses, mistakes, good advice, bad advice, joy, pain, disappointments, births, deaths and so much more. In each of these, there are levels of maturity. Are you the same person that you were three years ago or ten years ago? Have you made the same choices in the last three years? What have you done differently to get higher than you once were? Do you control your anger? Can you apologize and forgive quickly? Do you meditate on the things that have been done to you? If so, what are you saying and what is your resolve? Do you have a mentor? Who puts you in check? Are you even humble enough to submit to reprimanding? Measure yourself with the Word and how you LOVE God's people. Ask yourself: am I mature? Ask others you trust as well.

TO BE MATURE IS TO USE WISDOM INTERMINGLED WITH SELF-CONTROL, OMITTING FLESHY CHARACTER.

Supporting Scriptures:

- ◆ **Psalm 138:8 (KJV):** The LORD will perfect that which concerneth me: thy mercy, O LORD, endureth for ever: forsake not the works of thine own hands.

- ◆ **Ephesians 4:13 (NIV):** Until we all reach unity in the faith and in the knowledge of the Son of God and become mature, attaining to the whole measure of the fullness of Christ.

- ◆ **Hebrews 6:1 (NIV):** Therefore let us move beyond the elementary teachings about Christ and be taken forward to maturity, not laying again the foundation of repentance from acts that lead to death, and of faith in God.

Journaling:

Write down several words (at least eight) that are synonyms for maturity and utilize them in your speech, thoughts, reactions and responses at the end of the week.

Daily Reminders:

- Read the Word and ask for revelation.
- Hydrate with plenty of water/ lemons.
- Stay fixated on Jesus.
- Remember your fast and its purpose.
- Protect/guard your heart.
- Guard your ear gates and eye gates.
- Rest to preserve/conserve your energy.
- Mark prayer times on your calendar.
- Pray in tongues; this allows you to bypass your intellect.
- Always pray for your senior leaders.
- Repent daily.
- *Pray for one another.*

Impartation

Week Five, Day 38 (3 days)
LIQUIDS ONLY

Focus Point:

- Supernatural Impartation for a Future Shift/Birthing

Prayer:

King of Glory, we have denied ourselves for 38 days. We renounce our will. We ask for a divine supernatural impartation to do Your will, build You a house, and for wisdom, strength, prophetic insight and whatever the Holy Spirit sees that we need. We submit and receive it, in Jesus' name. Swell up in us today as we honor You and speak blessings over our new partners, team members, mindsets and our leaders constantly. We remember the faith on today and receive a supernatural overflow. Every evil intent, barrier, false way, and unseen principality is annihilated. Let this be the trimester of

birthing. We push in the spirit realm.
There will be no miscarriages or breached
births. In Jesus' name Amen.

Meditation:

There may be times when you are fasting,
praying, and standing in faith, yet you still
do not sense that anything is happening.
There are things that will occur through
the supernatural. Remember, there are
realms and levels in the supernatural.
While giving birth, it is important to listen
and hear at the same time. The correct
posture is important. Think of it as being
in alignment with God's will. You have to
agree to push when you are instructed to.
Your breathing will be labored, but the
Holy Spirit will be there to aid and guide
you. Jesus never left us without making
sure we were equipped. Labor and
contractions are simultaneous. Proper
meditation is an anecdote for a successful
delivery.

IMPARTATION CAN CATAPULT YOU INTO NEXT DIMENSIONS.

Supporting Scriptures:

◆ **Romans 1:11-12 (NASB):** For I long to see you so that I may impart some spiritual gift to you, that you may be established; that is, that I may be encouraged together with you while among you, each of us by the other's faith, both yours and mine.

◆ **1 Timothy 1:6 (NASB):** For some men, straying from these things, have turned aside to fruitless discussion.

◆ **Hebrews 13:7:** There is no record of Jesus ever healing anyone until He returned from the forty days of fasting that launched His earthly ministry. Jesus said we would do even greater works than He had done, because He was returning to the Father. If Jesus did not begin to minister before fasting, how can we?!?

Journaling:

> Write down a declaration for (Insert your church's name here). It does not have to be long.

Daily Reminders:

- Read the Word and ask for revelation.
- Hydrate with plenty of water/ lemons.
- Stay fixated on Jesus.
- Remember your fast and its purpose.
- Protect/guard your heart.
- Guard your ear gates and eye gates.
- Rest to preserve/conserve your energy.
- Mark prayer times on your calendar.
- Pray in tongues; this allows you to bypass your intellect.
- Always pray for your senior leaders.
- Repent daily.
- *Pray for one another.*

Demonstration

Week Five, Day 39

LIQUIDS ONLY

Focus Point:
- Demonstration/Finish with Tenacity

Prayer:

Father, we love You and provoke Your presence to invade our space. We honor You with our sacrifices, we honor You with gifts, we honor You with how we love one another. We have crucified our flesh and taken up our cross. We are positioned for more. Lord, we ask that You incline Your ear and that the essence of our prayers and worship is a sweet aroma that ascends to Heaven. Manifest every prayer that we have spoken in the last 40 days. Father, we pray that this journey that we have taken together will be honored. Let there be a birthing and a release. We ask for the spirit of knowledge, might, academia, and wisdom

as we teach and preach Your Word.
Demonstration shall be the portion of our church. This is the confidence that we have in You, that You have heard us when we prayed. In Jesus' name. Amen.

Meditation:

In closing the book of Hebrews, the writer tells us, "Remember your leaders and superiors in authority [for it was they] who brought to you the Word of God. Observe attentively and consider their manner of living (the outcome of their well-spent lives) and imitate their faith (their conviction that God exists and is the Creator and Ruler of all things, the Provider and Bestower of eternal salvation through Christ, and their leaning of the entire human personality on God in absolute trust and confidence in His power, wisdom, and goodness)."

DON'T CAST AWAY YOUR CONFIDENCE IN THE LORD, BECAUSE MAN WILL FAIL YOU.

Supporting Scriptures:

- **II Timothy 4:7-8:** I have fought the good (worthy, honorable, and noble) fight, I have finished the race, I have kept (firmly held) the faith. [As to what remains] henceforth there is laid up for me the [victor's] crown of righteousness [for being right with God and doing right], which the Lord, the righteous Judge, will award to me and recompense me on that [great] day—and not to me only, but also to all those who have loved and yearned for and welcomed His appearing (His return).

- **Acts 20:24:** But none of these things move me; neither do I esteem my life dear to myself, if only I may finish my course with joy and the ministry which I have obtained from [which was entrusted to me by] the Lord Jesus, faithfully to attest to the good news (Gospel) of God's grace (His unmerited favor, spiritual blessing, and mercy).

- **I Corinthians 15:58:** Therefore, my beloved brethren, be firm (steadfast), immovable, always abounding in the work of the Lord [always being superior, excelling, doing more than enough in the service of the Lord], knowing and being continually aware that your labor in the Lord is not futile [it is never wasted or to no purpose].

◆ **Philippians 4:10-14:** I was made very happy in the Lord that now you have revived your interest in my welfare after so long a time; you were indeed thinking of me, but you had no opportunity to show it. Not that I am implying that I was in any personal want, for I have learned how to be content (satisfied to the point where I am not disturbed or disquieted) in whatever state I am. I know how to be abased and live humbly in straitened circumstances, and I know also how to enjoy plenty and live in abundance. I have learned in any and all circumstances the secret of facing every situation, whether well-fed or going hungry, having a sufficiency and enough to spare or going without and being in want. I have strength for all things in Christ Who empowers me [I am ready for anything and equal to anything through Him Who infuses inner strength into me; I am self-sufficient in Christ's sufficiency]. But it was right and commendable and noble of you to contribute for my needs and to share my difficulties with me.

VICTORY

Week 5, Day 40

Eat light/Light soups

Focus Point:
- Defeat/ Victory/ Acquisition

Prayer:

God, You are the lifter of my head. I have fasted in hopes to kill my flesh and draw nearer to You. I have united with the Holy Spirit and other believers to touch and agree with every word that was spoken daily in the prayers and meditations listed in this book.

Meditation:

You have come to the end of another successful fast. If along the way you had to restart it, please do not badger yourself. God still loves you and you are still His choice. Abraham, David, Elijah and so many others did not do everything perfectly, but God never relinquished the ordained plans He had for them. Be excited for what is to come. There are some things you cannot see at the moment because you live and walk by faith. He will not reveal everything to you. Fasting breaks/eradicates darkness and crucifies the flesh. Take a deep breath and silence any negative opinion that the enemy has tossed at you. Be excited about your future and what the Father is doing through you. Lay hands on your belly and prophesy.

YOU DON'T HAVE TO OBTAIN WHAT YOU ALREADY POSSESS.

Supporting Scriptures:

◆ **Philippians 1:6:** For I am confident of this very thing, that He who began a good work in you will perfect it until the day of Christ Jesus.

◆ **2 Chronicles 15:7:** But you, be strong and do not lose courage, for there is reward for your work.

◆ **James 1:4:** And let endurance have its

perfect result, so that you may be perfect and complete, lacking in nothing.

Journaling:

What were some new things you learned while fasting that you can share with others?

Daily Reminders:

- Read the Word and ask for revelation.
- Hydrate with plenty of water/ lemons.
- Stay fixated on Jesus.
- Remember your fast and its purpose.
- Protect/guard your heart.
- Guard your ear gates and eye gates.
- Rest to preserve/conserve your energy.
- Mark prayer times on your calendar.
- Pray in tongues; this allows you to bypass your intellect.
- Always pray for your senior leaders.
- Repent daily.
- *Pray for one another*

YOU FINISHED WELL (GLORY TO GOD!)

You have endured and finished the race, and you will never be the same. Our focus now is to be one with the Father. I love each and everyone that has taken the time to journey with me. I decree supernatural miracles be bestowed upon you! Shalom!

End (telos):

To set out a definite point or goal; the point aimed at as a limit.

Journaling:

Write down any revelation that God has given to you during your 40 day journey.

Daily Reminders:
- Read the Word and ask for revelation.
- Hydrate with plenty of water/ lemons.
- Stay fixated on Jesus.
- Remember your fast and its purpose.
- Protect/guard your heart.
- Guard your ear gates and eye gates.

- Rest to preserve/conserve your energy.
- Mark prayer times on your calendar.
- Pray in tongues; this allows you to bypass your intellect.
- Always pray for your senior leaders.
- Repent daily.
- *Pray for one another.*

Udania J. Smith

A Prophetic intercessor, Psalmist and powerful communicator of the Word of God; this characterizes Udania J. Smith's ministry. She has been called to articulate God's infallible truths in ministry and in the marketplace. She is graced for the broken. Udania holds a Bachelor of Science Degree in Psychology and is pursuing her Masters in Mental Health

Counseling. She founded Innovence LLC Apparel in 2019, and she holds a licensure in cosmetology. She has delved into real estate to be able to represent the Kingdom and govern over land. She has mentored young girls with the Ladies of Virtue Mentoring Program in Chicago, Illinois; these young ladies were recently interviewed by Fox 32 Chicago. The framework of her ministry is undoubtedly a demonstration of supernatural gifts, prayer, and worship. For over 19 years, she worked in the healthcare industry at Northwestern Memorial Hospital in Chicago, Illinois.

Fatherless, broken, and a victim of domestic violence, Udania's passion for prayer, fasting and intercession was birthed through Wailing Women of God Ministries in 2006. She was discipled and trained under the tutelage of Pastor Linn C. Williams and served as an amour bearer for over six years. Udania's role consisted of outreach ministry at Haymarket Center, teaching sexual purity classes, ministering to the wounded, broken, and leading worship and prayer. She has also volunteered with Sonia Harper's Trauma Response Team in Illinois and has completed her certification in Evangelism at All Nations Worship Assembly in Chicago, Illinois. Prayer and fasting have become assets in her lifestyle. She now resides in Atlanta, Georgia, where she works for a real estate and wealth academy. Udania's love for people and her community is expressed in her servitude. Udania encourages people of all ages with her testimony and she inspires the hearts of individuals by exemplifying the love of Christ.